Parson
JACK RUSSELL

Parson
JACK RUSSELL
The Hunting Legend
1795 - 1883

CHARLES NOON

HALSGROVE · COUNTRY CLASSICS

First published in Great Britain in 2000
Reprinted in 2001

British Library Cataloguing-in-Publication Data
A CIP record for this title is available from the British Library

ISBN 1 84114 050 3

HALSGROVE

Halsgrove House
Lower Moor Way
Tiverton, Devon EX16 6SS
Tel: 01884 243242
Fax: 01884 243325
www.halsgrove.com

Printed and bound by Hackman Printers Ltd, Rhondda.

CONTENTS

PREFACE

To write a biography of Jack Russell needs no excuse. Everyone has heard of the terriers, and most have an idea that they were named after someone; this book is about that 'someone' after whom the breed of terriers was named. (No he didn't play cricket for Gloucestershire and England!)

This book is also written in the conviction that the Reverend John Russell was an important figure, both in the nineteenth century history of the West Country and indeed in the wider national perspective. The facts of his life may seem humdrum. Born in 1795 he was the son and grandson of Devon clergymen. Grandfather Michael was Rector of Meeth. His father, also called John, had a good eye for an opportunity, married well, and eventually held four parishes, Crediton, Iddesleigh and Jacobstowe in Devon and St Juliot in Cornwall. Russell himself received the conventional education of a Jane Austen parson – a public school, Peter Blundell's Grammar School in Tiverton, and then Exeter College, Oxford and was able enough to get along with a minimum of study and left Oxford with a degree but, like many another clerical Oxonian of the early nineteenth century, without any real scholarship. It has always been accepted that he bought the first of his terriers, called Trump, from an Oxford milkman.

His clerical career can be simply told: he served in four Devon parishes, South Molton 1820-26, Iddesleigh 1826-33, Swimbridge 1833-80 and Black Torrington 1880-83. The bulk of his time, forty-seven years, was spent at Swimbridge on the low stipend of less than £200 a year. He was never a 'pluralist' and, unlike his father, never milked the Church but, like his father, he married 'well'. The reader may follow me into believing that, in an unbigoted way, Russell was one of the great country parsons of his age, perhaps a little 'giddy' in his twenties, but maturing well at a time when the man or woman in the pew tended to despise Evangelicals and fear Anglo-Catholics. When a clergyman of the one or other persuasion immediately alienated a proportion of his parish, Russell was a plain Protestant who, sticking to the old ways, was much beloved by his parishioners. Both his bishops regarded him with favour, Henry Phillpotts only 'initially', but Frederick Temple 'continuously'. It is clear that he was a good man, that his parishioners loved him and that grief at his death was heartfelt.

But his fame was as a hunting parson who, unless ill or the weather inclement, hunted three days or more a week, every week. Russell was in his prime when the word 'Sport' meant hunting and Russell had a natural gift for the management of horse and hounds, understanding intuitively the wiles of the quarry, be it otter, hare, fox or deer. He was as brilliant a Master of Foxhounds as Garfield Sobers was a cricketer and to many Englishmen of his time he brought as much credit to his Church as the Reverend David Shepperd did when he opened for England. Russell became known, nationally as well as locally, as 'The Sporting Parson', was intimate with the Devonian landed gentry during the great age of their influence and in the last twenty years of his life became close to the Prince and Princess of Wales, without losing the common touch or becoming a snob. What other clergyman, from Devon or elsewhere has had a breed of dogs named after him, as well as pubs and a public school cross-country steeplechase? If I had a choice between either Russell or his contemporaries Keble or Newman to be my companion at the marriage at Cana I know whom I would choose!

In Russell's middle age it became part of the mid-century's canting humbug that hunting was OK for chaps and even for ladies, but not for the clergy. In Russell's youth most North Devon clergy, who could afford to do so, hunted, until Henry Phillpotts, who became Bishop of Exeter in 1830, conducted a vendetta against hunting clergy. But then he conducted vendettas against so many of his clergy.

Many may have heard the saying that 'Hunters be not holy men'. However it is not a biblical saying, being an invention of Chaucer's, who, in *The Prologue* to the *Canterbury Tales*, put the words into the mouth of his Monk. Hunters in the Bible are rarely mentioned, and actually get quite a good press. For example there was Esau, who was a straightforward chap, compared with his slimy and ruthlessly dishonest half-brother Jacob. The great biblical hunter of course was Nimrod, but all that is known of him was that 'he was mighty before the Lord'. Russell was educated within a system of thought that took the Bible to be literally and historically true and in the Bible there is no condemnation, or hint of a condemnation, of hunting.

Moreover for a hundred years after Russell's death in 1883 hunting was regarded as part of the traditional round of English life. It was something that contributed to the good fellowship of the countryside, helped keep landowners from being too often 'absentees' by giving them something to do in the winter and so contributing to local prosperity by ensuring that more of the rental incomes were spent locally. It is only in the last twenty years that attitudes have altered. As Lord Onslow put it on a recent *Have I Got News for You* programme 'In 1900 the Church of England was for hunting and against buggery; now it is anti-hunting and for buggery.' Fashions change and one wonders whether the anti-hunting phenomenon is a 'fashion thing' or a 'moral thing'. In an ideal world the fox would lie down with the goose or the lamb and all would eat grass together, but in a farming environment foxes (and deer) have to be controlled. They can be shot, gassed, poisoned, trapped or hunted. My own guess is that, if hunting is banned, farmers and landowners will exterminate foxes [and deer] by one means or another as an unmitigated nuisance. The paradox that the angler is the fish's best friend may well be true also in that, if hunting is banned, the 'hunter' may be proved to have been the rural fox's best friend.

Enough. I have enjoyed the writing and researching of this book. It began when I was out canvassing in 1981 and found an elector, Mr W. H. Mortimer, with some diaries of Russell's. (Appositely I was canvassing for the Liberals as most of Russell's politically active friends before mid century were all Whigs or Liberals, though his father was a strong Tory). Further diaries came to my notice at Hartland Abbey and Sir Hugh Stucley very kindly allowed me to use them and also to use 'The Poltimore Hunt' as an illustration. Ian Stoyle of Thorverton gave me valuable assistance in tracing Russell's ancestry and in correcting the errors of previous works in that regard. The staffs of the Devon, Cornwall, Hampshire and Somerset Library services have always been most courteous and helpful. Invariably the descendants of those with whom Russell hunted have been very welcoming, as have those who now own the houses which he used to visit. It is I think part of Russell's sweet memory that people of all walks of life have been so helpful. Sir Rivers Carew, a descendant of Sir Walter Palk Carew, lent me the letters that form a separate appendix. The Countess of Arran guided me to 'The Hermitage' on the Castle Hill Estate where Russell probably proposed marriage to Penelope Bury and very kindly helped my son photograph 'Snoopy', her very proper Jack Russell terrier. Mervyn Dalling, the chronicler of everything to do with Swimbridge, gave me permission to use his poems. Mr and Mrs Moore of Tordown and the current owners of Dennington allowed me to photograph their houses. Mr and Mrs Collins who own Russell's father's house in Calstock kindly sent a photograph. The Countess of Stockton kindly gave me access to St Hubert's Hall.

Another joy of writing this life of Russell has been the time spent in visiting the houses he lived and stayed in. Some of them still exist and are officially open to the public. The National Trust runs Dunster Castle, once inhabited by his Luttrell friends, a fantastic pile in a romantic setting and the stuff of legend. Some like Castle Hill at Filleigh are still lived in by descendants of the Fortescue neighbours of Russell in his Swimbridge and South Molton days. The houses of his wife's Chichester relatives, Youlston, Arlington and Hall, still survive in their park land, but Chichesters now only live at Hall in Bishop's Tawton. Colliepriest at Tiverton and Haccombe on the Teign are no longer Carew places, but are turned into flats. Most romantically melancholy are the stones of Eggesford, the Gothic palace, built by Newton Fellowes, later Earl of Portsmouth, on a spur overlooking the valley of the Taw, across the valley from Russell's wife's property of Colleton Manor, an exquisite gem of a house and only a few miles from the delightful hill top town of Chulmleigh, once the scene of such revelries. The ruins of Mark Rolle's massive pile at Stevenstone can be seen from Torrington. Both grand houses, Eggesford built in the 1830s, Stevenstone in the 1860s, were each destined to survive less than a century. Baron's Down, the home of the Stucley Lucas who was Master of Stag Hounds in the 1820s, overlooking the Exe valley to the east of Dulverton has been deliberately destroyed by its new owners, The League against Cruel Sports, to enhance the environment of the deer that Lucas chased. Charles Arthur Harris' mansion at Stowford has recently been rescued from dereliction and is once again a flourishing house, but its neighbour across the Tamar, Tom Phillip's Landue, is turned into flats. Visiting these places and the parishes Russell served has taken me to some of the most beautiful places in Devon, which is the same as saying to some of the most beautiful places in England.

And there are the moors and farmlands across which he hunted. Away from the roads Bodmin Moor, Dartmoor and Exmoor are as he found them, and, especially in winter, walking across them is to be part of timelessness. Exmoor was particularly Russell's home turf in later years and there can be few more exhilarating places to walk than from Dunkery to Brendon Common and down the Badgworthy, through the Doone country to Oare. Moreover the large empty country between the three moors, typified by his parish of Iddesleigh, is largely one that Russell would still recognise. No-one could be more privileged in his places of research than I have been.

A problem remains in presenting Russell's life to a wider public is that readers may not know Devon, East Cornwall and Exmoor as well as we who are privileged to live there. I have included a map of Devon with on it the main places and houses of his life. It is quite possible for readers with a modern 1:50,000 OS map to follow the runs described in this book, but quite impossible to produce maps within the parameters of this book to enable them to do so, as the distances were so great that the maps would have to be of the 'pull-out' variety.

Finally my wife is to be thanked for reminding me that I had been doing it for almost twenty years and was it not time to have finished? My children helped with accommodation so that I could economically use the London libraries. My son, Adrian Noon, and other friends helped with the photographs. Steve Goodwin, a colleague at Blundell's, deserves my thanks for photographing the 'Poltimore Hunt' and St Hubert's Hall, and Mr N. Swayne helped manipulate the text to production.

To them all are due a share of whatever merits there are; any errors are undoubtedly mine. Scholarly readers will deplore the absence of footnotes for which there is no real excuse except disorganisation and untidiness. However the sources of information are quite straightforward. Previous books are mentioned in the text. When Russell's own diaries are being used it is obvious. After 1830 the *North Devon Journal* proved to be a mine of information. The records of the parishes he served were often useful. It is in the nature of things that once this book is published more useful material on Russell will emerge, yet I am confident that no-one again will be able, like Hoskins in his great work on the history of Devon, to label Russell 'futile'. He was one of the great parish priests of the nineteenth century.

Chapter One

JACK RUSSELL'S FOREBEARS

'Jack' Russell's ancestry can be traced to a great-great-grandfather Dennys Russell of Falmouth who married Blanch Newman in 1659. Many of their offspring stayed in Cornwall, especially in Falmouth and St Gluvias, but one son, Michael, moved to Bideford where in 1702 he married Hannah Wren, who was both born and died in Bideford. Probably they had seven children, but only two sons, Denis, born in 1711 and the youngest child, Michael, born in 1718 survived into breeding adulthood. This Michael had the brains to profit from the teaching at Bideford Grammar School and went to Exeter College, Oxford as a 'poor scholar' in March 1737 of the old calendar. That he was a 'poor scholar' can be explained by his father's bankruptcy, which was reported in the London Gazette of January 1719: 'Michael Russel [sic] of Bideford, Tallow Chandler, Bankrupt. To surrender at the house of George Nation [Innkeeper] in Falmouth.'

Later tradition claimed that Jack Russell was descended from a nephew of the Lord Russell of the mid sixteenth century, who put down the Prayer Book rebellion of 1547, and was therefore descended from a branch of the Russells of Kingston Russell with arms and motto of *Che Sara Sara*, but, although it also appears under the entry for Michael in the Dictionary of Oxford Graduates, this seems fanciful and may have been an invention of Jack Russell's father. 'Poor scholar' was one of many categories of entry into Exeter College. Those who matriculated in 1737 were registered as 'gentleman commoners', 'commoners', 'sojourners', 'battellars', and 'P.S.', an abbreviation for 'poor scholar'. Of the 28 who matriculated with Russell in the year 1737-8 one was a 'gentleman commoner' paying £8, ten were 'sojourners' paying £7, eight were 'battellars' paying £6 and nine were like Russell 'poor scholars' paying only £4. 'Sojourners', or Commoners as there were often called, shared 'commons' in hall, 'battellars' lived move cheaply with their own accounts or 'battals' and the 'poor scholars' received their subsidised instruction as the price of waiting on the fellows and sojouners in hall and perhaps elsewhere. Twenty six of the 28 gave a Devon or Cornish place of origin, one gave Taunton and one London, but his surname was 'Fortescue'. Although Michael Russell earned his education the hard way, he may have had the opportunity to make useful contacts.

In 1700 Bideford was an important port. Tradition has it that Walter Raleigh imported the first tobacco cargo into England there and in the first half of the eighteenth century, according to Tedrake and Gribble, its two historians, Bideford imported more tobacco than any port except London. However after 1714 the Newfoundland trade, its other staple, declined, which may have contributed to Michael Russell senior's bankruptcy. This commercial vitality did not necessarily foster enlightenment. In 1682 the folk of Bideford brought the last successful prosecutions for witchcraft in England. A seaman, John Coleman testified that he saw three old women, Mary Trembles, Temperance Lloyd and Susannah Edwards meeting with a black-coated figure near the Rectory, not in itself significant except that the black-coated gentleman had a spiny tail and cloven feet. He heard them chant in suspiciously Gilbertian mode:

> Beat the water Trembles' daughter
> Till the tempest gather o'er us,
> Till the thunder strike with wonder
> And the lightnings flame before us.

Then one of the weird sisters, presumably Mary Trembles chanted alone:

> Mount water to the skies,
> Bid the sudden storm arise,
> Bid the pitchy clouds advance,
> Bid the forked lightnings prance,
> Bid the thunder angry growl,
> Bid the wild winds fiercely howl,
> Bid the tempest come again,
> Thunder, lightning wind and rain.

Coleman must have had an excellent memory to recall all this verse, but, according to Gribble, a frenzied mob pressed willing magistrates to commit them to Exeter for trial, where they were condemned and executed, so old they could not mount the scaffold unaided.

The year before the witches were killed, Lewis Stucley, another citizen of Bideford, was born and had his sex and connections to thank for not being similarly dealt with. Trained as a lawyer he left its practice and set himself to discover the 'quadrative of the circle and the secret of perpetual motion'. He also became such a hypochondriac that he never left his house and always had money washed before handling it. Being wealthy, piles of coin accumulated in his house around which he ceaselessly paced in his philosophical quests. He also followed the campaigns of the Duke of Marlborough, digging up his floors to recreate the sieges. His only recorded outing was to go to the Town Hall to take the oath of loyalty to George I, when he was reported to have worn a small, round, tarred hat and a beard of immoderate length. When he died his body was covered in vermin.

Just before Michael Russell Junior achieved his M.A., Whitfield became Rector of Bideford and lived as its Rector until 1783. He was as curious a cleric as can be conceived. He lost his temper with the Town Council and tried to throw their records out of a room attached to the church, for which he was taken to court and had to pay damages. He left a child unburied for months and once stopped a service because he thought some members of the congregation were laughing at him and came from the altar and roared at the people, 'I am as good as any five hundred West Countrymen and you are all cowards'. He refused the use of the Vestry Room to meetings of the Vestry and wrote many pamphlets, one of which attempted to prove that Pope had written the *Messiah*.

The parish of Bideford being unavailable, Michael Russell, not without controversy became Rector of Meeth. On the death of the previous Rector, his son, William Ley of Dolton, petitioned the Bishop of Exeter on March 7th 1748 claiming that he was the true patron of the living. Because a Richard Blinch of Bideford entered a 'caveat' the bishop held an enquiry at the Cathedral on October 12th 1749. To that enquiry a number of local worthies were summoned, who declared that 'Oxford University has the presentation this turn' and that the last presentation was by Edward Cary of Torr Abbey, but that his son George Cary had become a 'popish recusant', thereby losing his rights. One wonders if this was a sensitive issue so soon after the 'Forty-Five'. As a result Michael Russell became Rector of Meeth, although Meeth was not an Exeter College living.

Meanwhile his mother had died in 1740 and his father came in old age to live at Meeth for his death is recorded in the Meeth registers in 1756. In the same year Michael married Grace Allen, who was the daughter or widow of a Bideford tobacco merchant. She was probably born Grace Phillips of Poughill in Cornwall in 1714, whose first marriage had been to Joseph Allen in 1746. Grace and Michael may have had twins born in Bideford in 1757, but the only child born to them in Meeth was John Russell in 1760. It is not known where and when Grace died, but Michael died in Meeth, still its Rector in 1790. One suspects a sensible and convenient marriage between a forty something widow with some assets and a clergyman past his first youth.

Apart from the wildernesses of Exmoor and Dartmoor there can have been few places more cut off from the commerce of the world than Meeth in the mid eighteenth century. Its population in 1801 was given as only 257 and it stood on high ground above the Torridge, about half way between the twin townlets of Great Torrington and Okehampton each in 1801 just over 1500 in population. About halfway between Meeth and Okehampton is Hatherleigh described dismissively by John Swete on his travels in the 1770s as 'a very mean town'. Ten miles or more to the west lay the smaller 'town' of Holsworthy and a similar distance to the east the comparative 'city' of Crediton with, in 1801, almost 5000 inhabitants. To be educated John Russell first had to make the 15 mile journey to Bideford Grammar School, probably boarding with the Master and then in 1774, at the age of thirteen, going as a boarder to Blundell's School in Tiverton.

The great attraction of Blundell's for the education of the sons of such as Michael Russell was the munificence of its foundation by Peter Blundell, whose wealth and charitable bequests must allow comparison with the Nuffields, Wolfsons and Sainsburys of the twentieth century. The only certainty about Peter Blundell is his birth in Tiverton and the date of his death in London in 1601. After many other bequests had been met the residue of his will was to be spent on the setting up of a 'Free Grammar School' in Tiverton for 150 pupils, a school of immense size for 1601, when one reflects that many other schools had a mere 10 to 50 pupils. Blundell was quite clear in his will that it was to be free and 'not a school of exaction' and the accepted meaning of 'Grammar' was Latin and Greek. Later problems crept in from a conflicting provision that if the 150 places were not filled by Tivertonians then 'foreigners', i.e. non-Tivertonians, could be admitted with the consent of those ten Tivertonians who paid most tax. This of course meant provision for boarders. Blundell appointed as his executor Chief Justice Popham. If too little is known of Blundell, too much is known of Popham. It is curious that so wealthy a man as Blundell never married, but not so strange that so little else is known of him, as records and portraits were almost certainly destroyed in the Great Fire of London.

Popham married and set himself up in Wellington after a colourful career, which included a spell as a highwayman on Shooters Hill, being the prosecuting Attorney-General against Mary Queen of Scots and being the judge who condemned both Guy Fawkes and Raleigh. Perhaps the close connection of Popham and Blundell suggests that Blundell's fortune may have come from more than trade in woollens. Some of it may have come from government loans, monopolies and the vast perks then associated with government activity, which make contemporary sleaze seem very small beer.

The size and munificence of Tiverton Grammar School were only part of its attractions; as important were the scholarships to the Universities set up by Popham as part of his role as Blundell's executor. Popham made arrangements with Balliol College and Sidney Sussex College for scholarships and Fellowships for former pupils of Blundell's School, who had to be under nineteen years of age on election. The elections would be carried out by the 24 Feoffees appointed to oversee the school. A later benefaction by another wealthy Tivertonian, Ham, created more scholarships, but these were tenable at any college to which the pupil could gain admission. In the early nineteenth century further, Gilberd, exhibitions were set up, one of which was eventually awarded to Michael Russell's grandson. There were then many good reasons for the Rector of Meeth to send his only son to Blundell's.

In 1774, Russell's first year at Blundell's, Philip Atherton was still Master (Headmaster), but for the remainder of his time he was under Richard Keats. The Master still received the salary of £50 stipulated in Blundell's will, a generous sum in 1604 when the School had begun, but inadequate in 1774. The Usher, or Assistant Master for the Lower School, Thomas Wood, only received £20, and the poor old Porter, William Pottingham, who kept the gates and did odd jobs, like preparing a sufficient stock of birches, received £2-15s-0d. The masters made their living out of the exploitation of boarders and the charging for tuition for those subjects like mathematics, which were technically not covered by the term grammar, whose instruction had to be free. This is reflected in the terms used by the Clerk to the Feoffess when he recorded Keats' appointment, '… be elected and chosen Master of the Grammar School in Tiverton aforesaid in the room of Philip Atherton, who has resigned, and is to have £50 yearly with all other advantages and profits belonging to the said school-master'. In the 1770s pupil numbers fluctuated between 90 and 110, at least 80% of whom were boarders, the sons of clergy, 'gents', 'Esquires' and Baronets; there were very few Tiverton Day Scholars. This would cause problems later when the comfortable laxities of the

Ancien Regime were regarded with the cold eye of utilitarian reform.

John Russell probably flourished at Blundell's and had affection for his former Master, being one of those who subscribed to a commemorative portrait engraving of Keats when he died in 1812. Keats seems to have been a bit of a character, who gave each boy a sobriquet and who carried with him a knotted rope, called 'Discipline' with which he swished at minor defaulters such as those who had their feet on desks. It appears to have been his jest to threaten to hit a neighbour of the offender so that the real object of 'Discipline' should be unaware of the impending lash. Because of his previous experience at Bideford Grammar School Russell probably went straight into the Upper School, where he would have been instructed by Keats and, after 1776, by the Assistant Master that the Feoffees allowed Keats to hire for £10 p.a. He may have spent a token time in the Lower School under Mr Wood, about whom more is known because a fragmentary diary and account book of his have survived. They reveal a simple social life of cards for small stakes and some charitable giving. But he was an ageing man, who in 1787, in his sixties, had to resign because of ill health. Some naughty little boys, whose average age was about eleven produced a journal of what they called 'A New and Accurate History of the Rebellion carried against Thomas Wood commonly called Usurper By an Honourable Party of young man students of Blundell's School In the Glorious Year 1787. By a Person concerned. Second Edition corrected and revised.' It is useful for recording the sort of 'uniform' that Russell might have had to wear and for the flavour it gives of life on the banks of the Lowman, the river which flowed along two sides of Old Blundell's.

The affection in which Russell held his old school can be measured by the regularity with which he attended the annual 'Feast' held on St Peter's Day. He first returned in 1789, paying half a guinea for the occasion. The procession formed up in the School Green, at its head the Porter, Hezekiah Warren, William Pottingham having just died. The Porter was in his gown and staff. After the Porter came the Scholars, two by two, the juniors first. Then came the Master and Usher, followed by a 'band of music', the Old Boys, the Feoffees, the special preacher of the day, the honorary President of the Feast and the Stewards with white wands of office. From the School the procession would go up Bampton Street, turn left to St Peter's Church. Dinner was at the Three Tuns, an inn once near the present Post Office. After the feast the company made 'benefactions' including a vote of a shilling a week to the widow of Pottingham. For a School of barely 100 pupils the turnout was extremely good, varying from year to year between 60 and 100 and about half of them were the clergy of Devon. Russell was present in 1790 and 1791. As will be seen he was married in 1792 and did not grace the Feast with his presence again until 1795, when he was asked to be the special preacher of the day for 1796. He was elected a Steward in 1797 and he was present every year from 1790 until 1815 when the minute books cease to record the names of everyone who attended. Keats and Thomas Wood also came every year until their deaths. An especial occasion must have been the 200th Anniversary feast of 1804 when Philip Blundell, a collateral descendant of the founder, was the elected President.

In 1777 Russell was elected to one of the Scholarships at Sidney Sussex College, Cambridge, endowed by Peter Blundell in his will for the benefit of pupils from Blundell's School. The Account Book of the School records payments made to him of £9-0s-0d in October 1779, of £4-10s-0d in June 1780, of £9-0s-0d in August 1781, of £4-10s-0d in January 1782 and £4-10s-0d in October 1782, which at approximately £9 a year compares favourably with his father's £4 tuition charge at Exeter College almost forty years before.

Russell gained his B.A. in 1782, his M.A. in 1785 and was elected a Fellow of the College, not necessarily a mark of academic excellence in those days, as early as May 21st, 1783, but did not become effectively a Fellow until he had gained his M.A. at Michaelmas 1785. He resigned his fellowship at Lady Day 1792, when he married. His early career is curious. He reappears in the Devon records as receiving a Game License in Bere Ferrers, which was a populous parish at the tip of a peninsula between the Tamar and the Tavy. Between 1785 and 1791 it appears that he was curate of Bere Ferrers to the Reverend W. Short, a contemporary of his father's at Exeter College, who was also Rector of Thorverton. An arrangement seems to have been worked out between them. Between April and October every year Russell did duty at Thorverton and between October and April he went to Bere Ferrers, while Short spent the winters in Thorverton and the summers in Bere Ferrers. The Tamar in those days was a flourishing artery of trade, especially for the export of Cornish minerals and for the arming, provisioning and victualling of the fleet at Plymouth. Bere Ferrers itself profited from this late eighteenth century boom as its mediaeval silver mines were reopened in 1784, and in neighbouring Bere Alston up to a thousand miners were employed until activity declined after 1850. Further upstream at Calstock and Morwelham was the copper so essential to the copper-bottoming of the fleet. A very different and more vibrant world from that of Meeth, here on almost every reach of the Tamar great houses reflected the power and wealth of those whose grandfathers had not been bankrupt tallow chandlers: Mount Edgecumbe, Anthony, Pentillie Castle and Cothele.

In ways that we cannot now trace, Russell's residence at Bere Ferrers brought him into contact with the Terrells of Calstock, and in 1792 John Russell was married to Honor Terrell. On the wall of Calstock Parish church is a dignified memorial to 'Mr.' John Terrell of Higher Dimson, Honor's grandfather, who died in 1804 and to his son also John Terrell, 'merchant', of Halton Quay who had predeceased him in 1796 and who was Honor's father. The Terrells were obviously substantial. The area of Dimson lies to the north west of Gunnislake, the industrial suburb of Calstock, is obviously fertile and positively bristles with old mine chimneys and other workings, and Gunnislake is the highest navigable point of the tidal Tamar. Halton Quay is at the southern end of the parish of St Dominic and its trade may have been more agricultural, but agriculture was so prosperous in the Tamar valley during the Napoleonic wars that land values increased by a multiple of two and a half. In 1825 when Russell drew up a will, a draft of which is in the Devon Record Office, he refers to property inherited from his own childrens' grandfather, John Terrell as including land in St Dominic and Linkinhorne and sums in cash totalling over £7500, all in trust for the grandchildren. It was a good marriage at least for Russell, especially as his father-in law died so soon afterwards.

The entry in the marriage register of Calstock does not describe Russell as of Bere Ferrers or Thorverton, but as of Clifton, or Townstall, Dartmouth. I think the explanation lies along the following lines. Either with Honor's dowry or as a result of a gift from his father-in-law Russell, remembering how well Keats had done for himself at Blundell's, briefed an architect, Mr Salisbury, to build Belmont House, Dartmouth, intending to set up a school. In *Trewman's Post* of December 1st, 1791 he inserted an advertisement that a 'Grammar School' for six 'young gentlemen as boarders' was to be opened and that 'proper Masters would attend to teach Writing, Arithmetic, Music and Dancing'. It ended 'Mr Russell's terms are moderate, which, with other particulars, will be transmitted on application.' It appears that six or seven sons of gentry were educated at Belmont House. On the death of his father-in-law in May 1796 this mundane pedagogy became unnecessary and, as a further newspaper advertisement of October 1796 shows, Belmont House was put on the market. Otter Davies, writing a Memorial of Russell's life, whose source was the elderly Jack Russell, wrote that Russell kept hounds as well as pupils at Belmont and that his method of encouraging good work was to keep a hunter for the use of the pupil who achieved the highest marks. Davies continued, 'A

Cornish gentleman, whose father had been educated by the elder Russell, writes thus to the author of these memoirs: "My father has long been dead, but I can well remember the delight with which he was wont to talk of his schooldays in Dartmouth and the admiration he felt for his dear old master. Of him he would say that he was one of the best classics, one of the best preachers and readers, and by far the boldest hunter in the county of Devon. Not unfrequently too, my father would add, have I seen the fine old fellow's top-boots peeping out from under his cassock".'

It was at Belmont that the Russells' two oldest children were born, Nora in early 1793 and John in December 1795. The Russells moved back to Calstock after the death of Honor's father, and at Dimson they rebuilt and gentrified an older house called Sandhill. Between 1797 and 1808 Russell acted as curate of Southill, the mother church of Callington, but really a separate rural parish about 7 miles from Sandhill. He took his duties seriously enough to have his youngest children, Michael and William, baptised at Southill Church in 1797 and 1799. It is of course possible that he lived some of the time at Southill Rectory, but, as all accounts state that he built Sandhill, within easy walking distance of his grandfather-in-law's house at Dimson, it is more likely he lived in the livelier parish of Calstock. In 1804 The Earl of Mount Edgecumbe appointed him Rector of Dittisham, worth £540 a year in 1831, but he surrendered the incumbency in 1806 to a Mr Hutchinson. The Terrells had probably made him known to the gentry of the riverbank. Interestingly in the Tithe Apportionment Records of Calstock and the neighbouring parishes there is no mention of any land in the ownership of Terrells or Russells. The Dimson patrimony had been spent by 1840.

For whatever reason as he passed forty years old the patronage began to flow. His first accretion is the most curious. In 1810 he was appointed jointly by Francis Rawle and Arscott Molesworth of Pencarrow to the Perpetual Curacy of St Juliot, on the coast north of Bodmin. There is no record of his ever visiting the parish and the few duties that were done were performed by the curate of St Gennys. In 1812 these amounted to the great total of four baptisms and one marriage. According to Lake's *Parochial History of Cornwall*, Vol 2, he held the appointment until 1844 and in his reign the church fabric went to rack and ruin. 'Excepting the south aisle, extreme age has reduced this once superior church to a state of irremediable dilapidation' and as early as 1854 virtual rebuilding had been deemed necessary. Russell's reputation for stewardship might not have been so publicly impugned if the architect for the restoration had not been the young Thomas Hardy, who went on to marry the Rector's sister-in-law and to write a novel of the experience, 'A Pair of Blue Eyes', set in St Juliot.

Russell's next appointment was to become the Assistant Vicar of Crediton, to which he was elected by the 12 Governors of Crediton Church in 1811 and where he started officiating in October 1812. The only suggestion to explain this move is 'political'. In 1810 Britain seemed to the more nervous of the ruling classes to be on the verge of imitating the French and having a revolution. Towns like Crediton might become areas of sedition and Russell's Toryism could be relied on. An inquiry into election practices in 1818 records that Russell and R.H. Tuckfield, a J.P. and prominent local landowner who lived in Shobrooke, visited a voter, John Lamprey of the Prince Frederick Inn, and canvassed him on behalf of the Tory Sir Thomas Acland and against the Whig Lord Ebrington. Finding Lamprey unpersuaded, Russell, it was alleged, threatened Lamprey with the loss of his Licence. Russell was also later thought to have turned over a 'free trader' [i.e. smuggler] to the authorities. The account of the alleged blackmail of the publican is recorded in *Trewman's Flying Post* on June 25th, 1818 as having occurred earlier in the month on June 3rd. By its position and context it had been inserted in the paper by political opponents. Russell had earlier signed a pledge of support for the Tories Acland and Bastard, as had Tuckfield, who had also advertised a promise to assist voters to the poll at Rougemont Castle, Exeter. Ebrington came top of the poll with 4090 votes thanks to the unpopularity of the government and a well organised campaign to persuade Whig voters not to use their second vote, but to 'plump' for Ebrington, the supporter of Catholic Relief, the Reform of Parliament and the commutation of tithe. Russell was a sufficiently fierce Tory to be present at a meeting a fortnight after the poll to promise support for Acland next time, and his ally Tuckfield was appointed to the committee to re-elect Acland. During this 1818 election Admiral Bury of Swimbridge, whose daughter was to marry Russell's son, Jack, in 1826, was working for Ebrington and was sufficiently committed to the Ebrington cause to provide transport to Whig voters from Swimbridge, Landkey and Tawstock.

The Register of Oxford Graduates states that Russell was appointed Vicar of Burbage in Wiltshire and Vicar of Hurstbourne Tarrant in Hampshire, both in 1814, and that he held the former until 1841, but surrendered the latter in 1818, but this is a confusion with another John Russell, who was a master at Charterhouse. However it is certain that in 1823 Henry Hobhouse, a junior Secretary of State, presented him to the Rectory of Iddesleigh, and in 1836 the patron, Leonard Burton, appointed him to Jacobstowe. Quite a pluralist, but not to the extent that Foster would have us believe.

By the time his children emerged from the anonymous shadows of infancy their father, the Reverend John Russell, Vicar of Crediton, was well known locally as a staunch Tory in both Church and State. The newspaper coverage of the elections shows that he was on good terms with many of the gentry of the country to the north of Exeter, the Tuckfields, Aclands and Northcotes, and his regular attendance at the Blundell's Feasts suggests the cultivation of useful wider connections. He had married to advantage, and, although not rich, the family was comfortable. If these things matter, Jack Russell had been given a good start.

Chapter Two

JACK RUSSELL: SCHOOLBOY

The first certain information of his education is that Jack followed his father to Blundell's in October 1809, when he was rising fourteen years old. But it is known that he had already attended Plympton Grammar School, whose records are gone. It had been founded in 1658 and in its day it had had some fame as the educator of Joshua Reynolds, but it suffered from having as hereditary governors the Earl of Mount Edgecumbe and the Marquis of Lothian, who delegated their functions to local stewards; whereas Popham had established a group of 24 trustees for Blundell's School, most of whom were local worthies, knights, baronets, esquires and 'gents'. A government commission of 1868 reported that Plympton School was dilapidated, had only seven pupils and that 'the history of this school during much of the present century has been a continual series of calamities and misunderstandings'. Hine, in his *History of Plympton,* wrote in 1862 that the Schoolroom was 63ft by 26ft with the Master's desk at one end. 'Overhanging the entrance on one side is a small gallery approached from a chamber once used as a class or flogging chamber, but now too dilapidated for either purpose'. One wonders if County Councils nowadays when instructing architects on the specifications for a new school include a flogging chamber.

All that has come down from Russell's days at Plympton is the tale of a fight between him and John Crocker Bulteel, the son of Bulteel of Flete (in Holbeton). The story is told by Davies from Russell's reminiscences as an old man. Apparently Russell had been insulted by Bulteel and tore up one of Bulteel's books and a fight followed which Bulteel lost. Exactly at the same age as his father had been, Russell was sent to Blundell's and probably for the same reasons – the lure of the scholarships to the Universities.

In 1809 when John Junior entered Blundell's there had been changes of detail, but probably not of substance, in the running of the School. Firstly the masters had changed. The Master was now William Page Richards, who had succeeded Keats in 1797 and who was to remain as Master until 1823. He was the most successful Master of the Blundell's Ancien Regime, who inherited a school of 106 scholars and raised it steadily to a peak of over 200 in the post war boom of 1815. He was arguably the greatest flogging headmaster of his day and successful also in the sense meant by one of the Feoffees, Sir John Duntze, who opined that Richards had made £60,000 out of the school, an immense fortune. Richards also had clerical preferment, being presented to the Rectory of Stoke Abbas in Dorset in 1811 by his Oxford College. Whilst Richards presided in the Upper School, in the Lower School was the Usher, now John Ley who had been appointed in 1788 when Wood had resigned because of ill health. Ley resigned in 1823 in circumstances of adverse publicity when a parent sued him for allegedly causing a pupil to be permanently crippled because of the severity of a flogging, which publicity may have contributed to Richards decision to retire also. The Porter was now Hezekiah Warren, who had followed Pottingham in 1786. Life was not so good for Porters of Blundell's as he was still on his pittance of £2-15-0 a year plus use of the lodge and he was summarily dismissed in 1817, after thirty-one years service, 'in consequence of complaints against him for misconduct' (Meeting of the Feoffees, June 30th, 1817).

The increase of numbers was overwhelmingly an increase of boarders, which entailed the building of new accommodation and which produced wealth for the Master and Usher. In 1816 the Feoffees paid £80 to Richards towards the completion of an additional building to the Master's house and £30 to Ley for an additional building 'adjoining the parlour in his dwelling house'. Nevertheless the accommodation for 150 boarders was by no means generous and they slept two or three in a bed in those days; only in 1838 did the Feoffees agree to a plan which would allow each boarder his own bed. Plumbing was not good. The Master's House got the first water closet in the history of the School also in the 1830s, but the boys were still using privies that discharged directly into the Lowman as late as the 1860s.

The good living that the Master and Usher made was largely, but not totally, dependent on the profits of boarding as it seems that they turned a bob or two out of charging fees to Day Scholars as well. The evidence may be tainted as most of it comes from the depositions of hostile witnesses in the Chancery Case of the 1840s, when the Townsfolk, led by the post-1832 Liberal M.P. John Heathcoat, supported by the post 1836

Liberal Borough Council, tackled Blundell's, the last bastion of Toryism in Tiverton, on the multiple grounds that Peter Blundell's will was being perverted towards the benefit of 'foreigners', that day boys were being ill-treated, that fees were being charged to day scholars as well as to boarders, that 'foreigners' were being favoured against Tivertonians in the award of scholarships, that the education provided was inappropriate to the 1840s and that too many Feoffees lived away from the town.

Whether tainted or not the evidence is overwhelming and consistent. It seems that, as a boarder, Russell must have taken part in the daily persecutions of the socially inferior day scholars. By its nature the depositions of the 1840s usually refer to a time after Russell had left Blundell's and tend to refer to the 1820s and 1830s, but there is no reason to assume circumstances had changed much. Thomas Hurley, a day boy for only a few months in 1829 asserted that 'the ill treatment for which I left was, that having refused to go on an errand for a boarder I was placed before the fire until the skin of my face was very much burnt and afterwards a boarder threw a cricket bat at me with so much violence, as to break the bat and injure me so much that I was kept in bed for several days ... I think the Masters encouraged the boarders to use the day boys ill ... I can also state that a day boy by the name of Fisher was held with his head through the hole of the seat of a privy, with his heels just above the said seat until he was nearly suffocated.' With monotonous regularity each witness comments that the day boys were ill treated by the boarders. Thomas Adams, who had been the School's Writing Master from 1800-29 stated that he took his son away in 1825 because he had been cruelly beaten by a monitor. Probably in Richard's time the fierceness of his discipline kept some of the worst excesses in check.

But there was also bullying and violence amongst the boarders. Smaller boys were regularly taken to the school bathing place up the Lowman, where they were thrown into a deep pool, the current of the stream being relied upon to bring the gurgling small fry to a beach of shingle – this was called 'sheep-washing'. Bolstering was apparently also a common pastime. Older boys would place a victim on a bed and beat him with bolsters twisted and compressed to form a hard club. 'Cramping' was another custom which Russell may have had to endure. Once asleep a running noose would be fixed to the victim's big toe, the cord taken out of the room through the key hole of the door, the door re-locked and the gleeful tormentors would then heave on the cord. It is not difficult to assume a system where bullying and violence were endemic and normal. As F.J. Snell comments in his *Early Associations of Archbishop Temple*, 'There was no redress. The masters were a class apart.

They sat and heard lessons in the schools; they came into hall and heard prayers read on holidays; one of them, usually the headmaster, presided at dinner; and they came round to see that their charges were in bed. But there the connection ended. They took no part in the house-rule, the big boys saw to that' In the first part of *Lorna Doone*, Blackmore, a Blundellian between 1837 and 1843, describes the Blundell's, not of Ridd in the seventeenth century, but of his own time. Bullying and fighting were normal and the traditional place for fights was a triangle of grass, called the 'ironing box', almost under the Master's windows.

Snell was at Blundell's from 1877-81, a member of the last generation of boys to live in the old School Buildings, built by Popham beside the Lowman, at a time when nostalgia led many Old Boys to reminisce about the 'Good' Old Days. Such nostalgia has preserved knowledge of the daily routine. Reveille was at 6.30a.m. and the first schooling began at 7.00a.m. with a roll call soon after. Absences from the roll call meant the levying of a fine, which was deducted from the Sunday dole of pocket money. If a boy's fines outweighed his money he would be flogged. Schools lasted from 7a.m. to 9a.m., 10a.m. to 12 p.m. and 2p.m. till 4p.m. Most of the work was Latin and Greek and a daily task of Latin versification was set, a lesser amount of arithmetic and, if you paid, some dancing.

The food was grim. Walter Hook, at Blundell's in 1810-11, recalled that the teaching was indifferent, the discipline severe and the food scanty, and that he saved all his pocket money to buy buns and loaves. In a letter written home in February 1818, another Blundellian wrote, 'I went to School on Monday. There are two schoolrooms , one for the lower and the other for the higher classes; but there is no fire in them and we are dreadfully cold while there. [No heating in the classrooms until the 1830s, over two hundred years after the School was founded!] I am in the higher school in the third class below the head class. We sleep two in a bed no bigger than my little desk-bed at home. There are about one hundred boarders here. We have for breakfast a penny roll and about a teacupful of milk and water. We are only helped once at dinner; sometimes we get a good plateful, and at other times scarcely enough to feed a crow, just as it happens. We have a small piece of bread and butter or cheese for supper and a teacupful of beer. These are our meals. From what I have said you can judge how I am situated, yet I am as comfortable as I can expect to be in so large an establishment. You must not think, my dear mother, that I am unhappy here, for I shall be as happy as a prince when I have heard from you … I hope you will excuse the bad writing as I am in a hurry to send this letter by the evening post and consider that there are about a dozen boys playing and talking together.'

In a later letter the same boy gave a fuller description of life on the Lowman. 'You wished to know every particular of the school. I think it is a very good one and I trust I shall improve under Mr Richards' care. Tell Tom and Harry that Latin verse is a very essential requirement here as I have to do 20 lines a week, and two themes, an English and a Latin one every week. The books I read are Caesar, Virgil, Horace and Homer. As to Mr Richards, he is very careful of the boys, if they are unwell or have colds or anything the matter with them, so you have no reason to be anxious on that account. We can get into no mischief, even if we were disposed, which I hope is not the case, as we do not go outside the gates of the playground after three o'clock. Our names are called over at half-past seven in the morning, when everyone who is not in school forfeits twopence and stands a good chance of a box on the ear from Richards. They are called over again at nine when we have breakfast; at one, dinner; at six, supper; at eight, when we go to bed, – so that we are obliged to be pretty regular. We go to church twice a day if it is a fine Sunday, but the Sunday before last was so wet, Mr Richards read prayers to a numerous audience, as we were all there. We have prayers read every night before we go to bed by one of the monitors. We must be tolerably expeditious in getting into bed, because Mr Richards comes round in about two or three minutes after, and if we are not all in bed he is very angry. Sometimes the boys hear him come up, perhaps before they have pulled off their trousers, and when they try to jump in that state, they get entangled in them sometimes. If you send a box, I should like to have a neat penknife with two blades that is very sharp, and if you could send a hone to sharpen it upon and plenty of paper, as there is so much writing at this school that we fill three sheets of this sized paper [quarto] every week... If Tom has any books that he thinks will be useful, he might send them, such as Cornelius Nepos, Xenophon's Memorabilia or Cyropaedia. As for paying the postage, I think you need not do that as Mr Richards pays for them all and not the boys. Don't make yourself uneasy by thinking I am uncomfortable here, for it is not the case'.

The reference to the penknife and hone is interesting. A feature of Old Blundell's is that every piece of wall accessible to the human boy has been carved upon. Generations of boys have carved their names on the face of the building and every stick of furniture that has survived from Old Blundell's has been similarly treated. Some of that furniture even bears traces of having suffered a 'winkey'. A 'winkey' was begun by digging out a hole in a desk with the circumference of the hole dug deeper than its centre. Then a handful of saltpetre was put around the deeper parts of the hole and onto the raised centre of the hole would be placed a candle. When the candle flame burnt down low the saltpetre would be ignited and with luck might burn a hole right through the desk.

Of the education he received Archbishop Temple, a Blundellian of the 1830s, later said: 'I have sometimes thought that we might have been taught a little more than we were, and have wished that the course was a little wider than it was, yet I have never been able to get rid of the feeling that, if you have a few lessons and a great deal of time, to those who, like myself, took a great interest in the work, you found an incentive in the freedom in which you were left. I know I read the whole of Euripedes in my spare time. You may depend on it there is a real and special value in thus throwing a boy on his own resources, and allowing him to learn in such a way as that'.

On the other hand a boy constituted as Russell was would have used his abundant spare time quite differently. Three separate incidents have been preserved of Russell's activities at Blundell's. The first concerns a feud between Russell and another boy called Hunter. According to Otter Davies, Russell had been victimised and bullied by a monitor called Hunter, and got his own back by exploiting an edict by Richards that all rabbits and other pets were to be removed at once. Hunter kept pedigree rabbits and was slow to obey the Headmaster's orders, so Russell put some ferrets in the hutch to sort the rabbits out. This account needs correction because the Blundell's register reveals that, although Hunter came to Blundell's two years before Russell, he was two years younger than Russell. What is probably true is the rest of the story, that Hunter told Richards who gave Russell the thrashing of his life, probably with a riding crop.

Another tradition has it that Russell and a contemporary called Bovey began hunting a pack of dogs from School. It started from the great amount of unsupervised time that they all had, and Russell and Bovey spent much of it joining the farmers ratting and rabbitting. From this he and Bovey progressed to keeping a few dogs, housed with a blacksmith on the edge of town and, according to Otter Davies,'These were glorious days so long as they lasted; the farmers to a man, seeing the hounds chiefly managed by Russell, giving them a hearty welcome over their land, and supporting them in various ways calculated to show their cordial interest in the welfare of the pack. One, for instance, would say, 'he'd got a hare sitting in fuzzy-park bottom, and ef Maister Rissell wid on'y bring up his cry, he'd turn un out, and they'd have a rare crack o' hunting, sure enow.' Another would inform him that 'his auld blind mare had mit with a mishap, got stogged in th' head, and Maister Rissell was kindly welcome to her fer the dags'. Then there was no end to the bread-and-cheese and cider, which the hospitable and hound-loving yeomen of that county pressed on him and his companions, whenever the chase led them within hail of their farmsteads. Perhaps the happiness of a schoolboy was never more complete. Being a fair classical scholar, and gifted with more than average abilities, which in any profession might have carried him, but for his devotion to hounds, to the top of the tree, he found no difficulty in satisfying Mr Richards' class requirements and, at the same time, whenever a half or whole holiday occurred, in following the pastime he so keenly loved. But dark clouds were now looming in the horizon, portending a short season and disastrous end to this enjoyable life. Someone purporting to be a friend to good discipline wrote to Mr Richards, and communicated the astonishing intelligence that a cry of hounds was kept by his scholars, Bovey and Russell, and that the latter, if not sole manager, was at least the huntsman to the pack.

'Ringleader of the hunting gang' exclaimed Richards indignantly. 'What! set my discipline at naught and bring discredit on the honoured name of Blundell?' He sent for Bovey and expelled him on the spot. Russell came next, little doubting he should share a similar fate. 'You keep hounds don't you?' demanded the autocrat in a stern and pitiless tone.

'No, sir.'

'Do you dare to tell me a lie? Bovey has just told me that you do keep them,' said Richards, striking him with great violence. 'Tis no lie, sir,' pleaded Russell, pathetically; 'for Bovey stole them yesterday, and sent them home to his father.' 'Then that's lucky for you,' responded the Doctor, 'or I'd have expelled you too.' Unfortunately for the story it does not seem that Bovey was expelled as he left Blundell's on December 16th 1812, rising nineteen years old. And as he was almost two years the older, Bovey was probably the leader.

'These were glorious days'; this was Russell in old age reminiscing. His loyalty to the School which lasted to the last years of his life, when as an octogenarian he is to be seen in Founder's Day photographs, was built on this enjoyment. Bullying , fighting like Jan Ridd in the Ironing Box, the traditional site of bare knuckle bouts to the school boy death right outside the main door of the School, the blissful freedoms of those days innocent of the tyranny of organised games, the fishing, swimming and hunting, the fights with town cads, the lessons in the Upper School, already seeming of immemorial age, with its rafters [falsely] associated with the defeated Armada, the carvings of generations of names, the winkeys and the crampings and the vivid anarchy of schoolboy society must have been intoxicating to a social 'winner' like Russell. Every summer there were two events that probably held a bit of magic.

Every May 29th the School celebrated the escape of Charles II from the battle of Worcester, Oak-apple Day, by sallying forth into the country-side and cutting down greenery and small trees with which to decorate the Upper School to the rafters. The largest of the branches was dangled on a rope and under it would be seated the Master and before him each boy would declaim at least twenty lines of verse. In Russell's time the most popular piece was ' The Burial of Sir John Moore'. The rest of the day seems to have been taken up by 'sports', not the boring sports that happen on Sports Days now, but 'fun' sports like jumping for 'treaclers', i.e trying to eat sticky buns hung above your head with your hands tied behind your back, the buns being smeared with feathers as well as treacle. Dipping for coins in a bucket full of water and trying to get them out in your mouth. Donkey races, sack races and jingling. Jingling was fun. It consisted of forming a circle of up to 20 blindfolded boys surrounding one un-blindfolded boy armed with a hand bell. Using his bell it was his task to confuse the blindfolded seekers and to escape capture for as long as possible.

Every St Peter's Day, June 29th, the Feoffees met to make whatever decisions had to be made, and with them came a gathering of Old Boys to process to St Peter's Church, hear a sermon and have a feast. The older Russell, now Vicar of Crediton was a regular attender and, building on connections made in his Thorverton days, perhaps quietly insinuated himself with the Feoffees, who had the power to decide who would be awarded one of the closed university scholarships. In 1814, when Russell was eighteen, the Feoffees met, no doubt to award Russell the vacant Gilberd Exhibition worth £30 a year. However there was a hitch, only 11 Feoffees arrived and 14 were necessary for a legal quorum. They had to adjourn, fixing the 25th August 'for the purpose of electing an Exhibitioner as one of the candidates will be superannuated before the next general meeting'. Russell would be nineteen and therefore 'super-annuated' in December 1814. No meeting of the Feoffees happened in August, which must have been anxious for the Russells, but they did meet on 25th October and duly elected 'John Russell, son of John Russell of Crediton to the second Gilberd Exhibition'.

Interestingly it was not quite as straightforward as the Feofees' minutes suggest. One of the complaints of the Liberal Townsmen against the Feoffees in the 1830s and 1840s was that they favoured for-eigners against Tivertonians in their award of the precious scholarships. In support of the Town's case James Sellick, aged fifty-one, deposed that 'I recollect that about thirty years ago when I was about twenty years of age a young gent of the name of Russell, who was a son of the Rev. John Russell of Crediton and a boarder at Blundell's School, came to my father who was an inn keeper at Tiverton, and let out horses for hire, on the morning of a day on which an election was to be held for a scholarship, and requested my father to send some confidential person immediately to Sir Stafford Northcote at Pyne's House, who was one of the trustees of Blundell's School, with a letter which he said was to request Sir Stafford Northcote, as a friend of his, to come to Tiverton to attend the School Meeting which was of importance to him as he was a candidate in the scholarship, and the messenger was to ride fast, and my father sent me with the said letter and I took it to Sir Stafford Northcote and delivered it to him at Pyne's House. He immediately on receiving it ordered his carriage and came to Tiverton. I heard afterwards that the said young Mr Russell succeeded at the said election.' The Feoffees' minutes record that the meeting of October was attended by only the barest minimum quorum of 14 out of 24, which 14 included Sir Stafford Northcote.

So John Russell, son of the Reverend John Russell of Crediton went to Exeter College, Oxford with a Blundell's Exhibition, but like another more famous event of 1815 it had been 'a damned close thing', with Sir Stafford playing the role of Blucher. However the Exeter College records reveal that Russell came up with a Reynolds Exhibition. There were six of these awards founded by the father of Sir Joshua Reynolds; three were at the disposal of Eton and three of the Chapter and Chamber of Exeter, tenable until their holders were twenty-four and were designed to assist clergy to complete their education, preferably at Exeter College. The story that Russell spent the first instalment of his Gilberd Exhibition on the purchase of a horse then becomes more plausible if John Junior had two awards.

Like his father he retained an abiding affection for his old school, regularly attending the Feasts until their eclipse in 1850. He was first a Steward in 1824 and was asked to be the preacher in 1831. His brother William came to Blundell's in October 1814 and left, aged eighteen on St Peter's Day 1817. John Russell also sent his son Richard Bury Russell in 1840, but he left to go to Harrow in 1841. A contemporary described Richard Bury as 'slack-minded' so perhaps Harrow was more suitable. In due course he also continued the family tradition of bankruptcy. 'Jack' Russell was very gratified when, in 1877, the School's annual cross-country race was named 'The Russell' in his honour.

Armed with a basic knowledge of English history, some mathematics, as much dancing, the ability to write in a clear hand, a lot of Greek and Latin and a growing love for the chase, Jack Russell left for Oxford.

Chapter Three

FROM EXETER COLLEGE TO THE CURACY OF SOUTH MOLTON

Russell left Blundell's at the end of the summer term in 1814, immediately after the St Peter's Day Feast and Procession. He spent July, August and September at Crediton or thereabouts in his father's house, taking part in whatever sociability the local society of clergy and gentry would provide. I doubt if any nineteen year-old would willingly seek to spend the summer months at Crediton today, but Jack's father, with his Thorverton past would certainly have made himself agreeable to the neighbouring gentry, the Hippisleys of Shobrooke Park, the Ferguson-Davies of Creedy Park and the Bullers of Downs. A few miles away on a good road were the amenities of Exeter and the society of the Close. Towards the end of August there was the attraction of stag hunting. It seems that his father sent him to Tiverton Fair to buy a horse and he was conned by an experienced dealer into buying a two-year old, thinking it was a five-year old. On this raw beast he hacked on to Dulverton and joined a meet on September 20th at Stucley Lucas' house, Baron's Down. There he expected to find his father's groom with a fresh horse. Otter Davies reported the day thus: ' an awkward incident occurred that checked, and might have termi-nated, our hero's career before he had gone ten strides with the hounds. Mr Stucley Lucas, who at a later period became Master of the Stag Hounds, was riding a racehorse called Erebus and, as that gentleman was known to be an authority on all matters relating to the moor and the running of the deer, Russell very naturally looked to him as the pilot for the day. The racer, however, appears to have had little fancy for Jack's company for he was kicked under the stirrup iron with such force that he was thrown headlong to the ground'. This parted him from Lucas and 'now making the best of his way to Hawkridge, from the high ground of which he could view the hounds driving hard, and the field following at a long distance from him; and, just as he was about to start in pursuit, a gentleman trotted up from the opposite direction and counselled him to remain where he was.'

Comprehending intuitively that the stranger spoke with authority, Russell eased his mare along the ridge as he feasted his eyes on the wild and stirring scene taking place on the opposite moor. Russell's patience as a looker-on was not long tried; for even now the heads of the leading hounds were turning towards him, and he could distinctly hear the deep chop of their musical tongues, as, sinking the valley near Tarr Steps, they crossed the Barle and pointed directly for Hawkridge Moor.

Jack was now in his glory, alongside them on a willing steed, and they tearing ahead over the purple heather, as if on the very haunches of their game. With a trimming scent and never a check, it lasted for three long hours, when the deer, to baffle the pack, took soil under Slade Bridge, sinking himself in a deep pool and allowing little more than his nostrils to appear above the wave.

But the stratagem availed him not a rush; some five or six couple of old hounds dashed into the stream, and swimming in full cry, passed over him at first for a hundred yards or more; when James Tout, the huntsman, turned the pack, and then casting them steadily back, they winded him in his retreat. Every hound was at him in an instant, and a gambol of porpoises in that moorland stream could scarcely have created a greater commotion. 'There stood the stag, beneath them in the stream', writes Charles Kingsley, who must have witnessed a similar turmoil, 'his back against the black rock, with its green cushions of drip-ping velvet, knee-deep in the clear amber water, the hounds around him, some rolling and tossing and splashing in a mad half-terrified ring, as he reared in the air on his great haunches, with the sparkling beads running off his red mane, and, dropping on his knees, plunged his antlers among them with blows that must have brought certain death if the yielding water had not broken the shock'. Russell plunged into the water to assist at the kill and was after duly blooded in the presence of Earl Fortescue, who was the Master of Stag Hounds from 1812-18 and who would entertain the cream of the Field at Castle Hill after the day's sport. Apparently it was the custom when a good stag had been killed for James Tout to enter the dining room at Castle Hill in full costume, horn in hand, and sound a Mort, after which the assembled company would solemnly raise the toast 'Success to Stag-Hunting'. Later in 1876 the old Russell, dining at Castle Hill, was asked by the grandson of the Master of 1814 when he had first hunted the stag. Russell is reported to have told the then Lord Ebrington that it had been on September 30th,

1814 adding 'We found him in Padwells and killed him on the Barle under Slade Bridge. And there he is', he said pointing at the head and antlers of the very animal adorning the wall.

In the late Autumn of 1814 he quit Devon and went up to Exeter College, matriculating on November 9th. He graduated with the lowest form of degree on December 15th 1818. His ordination papers record that the relevant dons were prepared to certify that he had attended the requisite courses of lectures. In *Headlong Hall* Thomas Love Peacock has his hero, a Welsh Squire, who, on coming into his inheritance having a taste for improvement and wishing to fill his ancestral hall with 'philosophers and men of taste', set off for Oxford to find some. But on arriving at Oxford he met a learned professor who assured him that neither the one nor the other genus was to be found within the University. Russell, too, did not use his time at Oxford in the pursuit of unnecessary scholarship. But he made some useful friends. There was John Denne, unusual in being a Kentish Gentleman Commoner of Exeter, an Old Etonian contemporary of Charles Arthur Harris of Hayne, Stowford in Devon, of whom much more anon.

Denne introduced Russell to boxing and Russell took lessons from a professional, Rowlands, who coached pupils in the noble art in Denne's rooms. In a town and gown riot Denne had knocked down a prize-fighting butcher and, by the standards of the time, was an obvious luminary of the University. There was another Gentleman Commoner of Exeter, Gordon, who tended to mix with a Christ Church set, perhaps because Exeter was rather drab, and who was unpopular with the Denne-Russell gang. An exchange of words one evening in Hall led to a challenge that the best of Exeter could out box the best of Christ Church. The match was arranged in Denne's rooms, Russell boxed first and beat his opposite number into submission, while Denne polished off both the other House men and then gave the assembled and partly battered company a demonstration bout with Russell, whom he walloped. The falling Russell knocked over a table, breaking a receptacle which contained love letters addressed to Denne. One wonders why Russell remembered this detail to regale it to Davies so long afterwards. In attempting the biography of a man from whom few intimate papers have survived it is tantalising to wonder what his sex life was. Russell remembered Denne's letters, when he wrote about girls in his brief diaries he dropped into Latin, yet he married and fathered two children, so perhaps it is possible that his extraordinary hunting activity was some sort of sublimation. No conclusion is possible.

Apart from pugilism we know that he hired horses and hunted.

Denne it appears often travelled to Bicester and elsewhere to watch the big boxing matches, but Russell was sufficient of a West Countryman to prefer the wrestling of Cann or Polkinghorne. Apart from the boxing match with the Housemen all that is recorded of Russell's Oxford days is that he hunted with the Duke of Beaufort's hounds, with the pack of Sir Thomas Mostyn and with the Old Berkshire whose master was John Codrington. It was a Lincoln College man, Peter Jackson , who first encouraged him to go to a meet of the Heythrop at Sandford Brake. They hired two horses which they sent on ahead with two grooms to overnight at The Chequers Inn. At the meet they encountered the usual host of bloods, Mr Rawlinson, the owner of a Derby winner, Mr Lindo who was a sporting hero of the time at a time when the words 'sporting hero' invariably meant a 'hunter' and Sir Henry Peyton. However Will Long, the Duke's huntsman came to announce that the frost was too hard for the pack to come out. Will Long died at a good age in 1877 and, in later years, when Russell and he were riding back to Badminton after a hard day with the hounds they recalled the event, both of them remembering that Russell had been so disappointed with the announcement of the day's cancellation that he had exclaimed: ' Then I hope when you get back that you'll find them all dead on their benches.' Just the sort of thing a cocky undergraduate might have said.

Denne and Jackson were both Gentleman Commoners, as was Philip Dauncey another undergraduate with whom Russell hunted. Apparently a day in Dauncey's company remained 'etched for ever on the tablet of Russell's memory'. Hunting with one pack they were drawing a spinney near Bletchington House when the fox they started was also picked up by the Duke of Beaufort's hounds and away went both packs across the Bicester Vale. Most of the field failed to make a successful crossing of the Brook and Russell was one of the few in at the death along with such grandees as Lord Jersey, Sir Henry Peyton, Captain Evans and Tom Wingfield, to the general reader meaningless names, but to the keen sportsman of yesteryear as famous as Bradman, Hobbs and W. G.

As hunting is an issue these days, Russell's thoughts on the Christ Church drag hunt may be of some interest. To Otter Davies, Russell quoted, with approval, the sentiments of an Oxford horse-hirer, 'Squeaker' Smith who usually refused to hire out his horses to the drag riders on the grounds that 'Tisn't hunting, nor tisn't hacking; but, to speak plainly, 'tis barbarous cruelty to a noble animal'. The drag had none of the checks and pauses of the real chase and just degenerated into a flat out gallop over the country, with exhausted horses returning to stable covered in thorn splinters.

According to Otter Davies' account it was in Russell's final year that he bought a terrier, 'Trump', from a milkman while out walking towards Marston. Davies records that an oil painting of Trump existed in the possession of the Prince of Wales. Trump 'was white with a patch of dark tan over each eye and ear, while a similar dot, not larger than a penny piece, marks the root of the tail. The coat was thick, close and wiry, well calculated to protect the body from wet and cold. The legs are straight as arrows, the feet perfect; the loins and conformation of the frame are indicative of hardihood and endurance; while the size and height of the animal may be compared to that of a full grown vixen fox.' This Trump was the ancestor of all Russell's terriers, which were designed to chivvy the fox from its refuge and to be able to keep up with the field and capable of covering up to 20 miles in a day. Russell's terriers were longer in the leg than the present so-called 'Jack Russell' and illustrations suggest that the tail was not docked, or only half docked, so that if they got stuck underground the tail could be grasped to assist extraction, a working dog rather than a lap dog.

Eventually Russell achieved a degree. He was at Oxford soon after the system of 'Classes' had been introduced and the records show that he took his exam at the last possible moment, December 15th, 1818 and achieved the lowest possible Pass Degree, a Third. Four years spent within range of some of the best hunts in England probably had more influence on the undergraduate than any lectures or libraries. He had also met many who would play a large part in his later life, such as Charles Arthur Harris of Hayne near Stowford and John Templer who was a contemporary at Exeter College and the brother of George Templer, the eccentric owner of Stover, the nearest Devon came in the 1820s to a Hell Fire Club.

Meanwhile his father had been busy mapping out his son's first steps as a clergyman of the Church of England. Son John was ordained deacon in 1819 and priested in 1820 by George Pelham, the Bishop of Exeter in the Chapel Royal in London, a long and expensive journey away from Devon. The Ordination Records contain the usual documents – two from Oxford University. One was signed by van Mildert, later Bishop of Durham, then Regius Professor of Divinity, certifying that Russell had attended a course of his lectures in 1818. The other was from Exeter College couched in the usual half truths of academic references and confirmed Russell's residence at the College and reported Rusell as 'pie, sobrie et honeste vitam suam instituisse'. But the record contains two letters from Russell's father. The first nominated Russell to the curacy of St Juliot at thirty guineas a year. Initially Russell senior had entered the name of Charles Woolcombe of Jesus College,

Cambridge, but had crossed it out and replaced Woolcombe's name with his son's. The second letter from Russell Senior is to a cathedral dignitary who was organising the ordinations. It requests that the appointment to St Juliot is forwarded to the Bishop in London, explaining that his son will be doing duty partly in South Molton, partly in George Nympton, but that Mr W. M. Stawell, being only the Curate of George Nympton cannot appoint his son to the curacy necessary for ordination. Thus he cannot change the letter appointing his son to St Juliot 'with any truth and honour'. He ends by expecting the Bishop will agree to this unusual procedure as it would be 'a triple accommodation and entail no inconvenience to the Bishop'. So it was that Russell was ordained to the curacy of St Juliot, but never did duty there. W.M. Stawell had been an older contemporary of Russell senior at Blundell's and, according to Bishop Cary's Visitation of 1821, had been Curate of George Nympton, but resident in South Molton, for forty years. Bishop Cary's Visitation also lists Russell junior as Curate of South Molton with an income of £100 a year. The Rector of South Molton was the Rev. W. Toms, who was also Rector of Combe Martin, and he spent half the year in each parish, paying the Rev. William Mules £50 for being curate of Combe Martin. Mules also earned £25 for being curate of Instow. Mr Toms arrangements are curiously similar to those of Russell Senior's first rector William Short, who spent half the year at Bere Ferrers and half at Thorverton.

It is not surprising that Jack's father chose South Molton as the starting point of his son's career. It was not far from his grandfather's parish of Meeth and the ancestral town of Bideford. Moreover from 1816-20 William Moggridge Stawell was Mayor of South Molton, to be succeeded in 1820 in that office by James Riccard, who had married Jack's older Sister Nora at Crediton in January 1816. Their first child, Russell Martyn Riccard, was baptised at South Molton in January 1817 by his grandfather. Twins were born and baptised in November 1818, a further child was born in January 1820. James Riccard, a lawyer by profession, was often re-elected Mayor and his son Russell Martyn was Town Clerk from 1861 to '79, being succeeded in the post by his son Russell Louis Riccard. On arrival Jack would have important friends.

In the early 1820s the South Molton area abounded in curious accommodations. The parishes of Meshaw, Mariansleigh and Romansleigh were all in the hands of absentee rectors and their combined populations of 666 were served by the Rev. John Huxtable, another former pupil of Peter Blundell's School, who was also the Latin master at South Molton Grammar School, a puny establishment for a dozen pupils. In replying to Bishop Cary's questionnaire Huxtable affirmed that every

Sunday he did duty at each parish and in the summer months held two services at Romansleigh and that he performed Communion four times a year in each place, with 12 communicants at Mariansleigh, eight at Meshaw and 16 at Romansleigh. For his exertions Huxtable was paid £35 by the Rev. William Staback, rector of Mariansleigh, but resident in Exeter, £30 by the Rev. William Tanner of Romansleigh, also residing in Exeter and £45 by John Messiter of Romansleigh who was Garrison Chaplain of Woolwich.

Elsewhere in the neighbourhood the clergy had come to similar cosy arrangements. The Rev. William Karslake, Rector of Dowland for £40 served as curate of Dolton for the Rev. Henry Northcote, who was also rector of Monkokehampton, which was served for £40 by the incumbent of Winkleigh. Northcote lived in Swimbridge and was the Perpetual Curate of Swimbridge and Landkey and he also served as the Rev. J.B. Karslake's curate for Filleigh. Perhaps the nicest revelation of early nineteenth century clerical standards was the response to Cary's questionnaire by the Rector of Goodleigh, who was also Curate of Bittadon. In reply to Question XVI, an omnibus inquiry about difficulties in the discharge of duty, defects and abuses, he wrote: 'The regular duty of a country parish being a straightforward business, I have never experienced any difficulty in its performance.' However his reply to Question XIII about the state of the fabric had been: 'In my opinion the query may be answered in the affirmative – except the fabric of the Church; I very much doubt the safety of the building.'

Russell was not going to start his career as a clergyman of the Church of England in a very demanding milieu.

Chapter Four

BACHELOR PRIEST

T he registers of South Molton church record that Russell arrived in early 1819, taking a wedding on the April 4th, a funeral on the 6th and a wedding on the 9th. In May he took a service at George Nympton. Initially he was not overworked. In 1819 he performed 25 baptisms, a similar number of funerals and a few marriages, Stawell did rather more and Toms rather less. In 1821 and 1822 no less than ten clergy shared the work. One cannot be sure where he lived; perhaps he stayed with his brother-in-law, Riccard, perhaps in the Rectory, which he would have had to share with Toms for at least part of the year, perhaps he took lodgings.

In his first years at South Molton he suffered two tragedies. In June 1820 his mother died and in November 1820 his sister Mrs Riccard died aged twenty-seven. From the parish register we learn that the Riccards' address was the somewhat depressing 'Churchyard'. So far research has not found where Jack Russell's mother was buried, it was neither Crediton nor South Molton and the only evidence for her death is a one line notice in *Trewman's Post*.

In the 1820s South Molton was a T-shaped, hill-top town of terraced streets with a population of 3000 which was rising to a peak of 4482 according to the census of 1851. It had the remains of a cloth industry, it was a market for the surrounding area and such prosperity as it may have had may have been assisted by the periodic interest in mining on the southern slopes of Exmoor a few miles to the north. When Russell was curate, before the railways arrived in the 1850s it was an important coaching centre, with its main inn, The George having a brisk trade. Until the salutary reforms of the Municipal Corporations Act of 1836 it was governed by a self perpetuating oligarchy of eight members, whose main activity seems to have been entertaining themselves and their friends. After the 1836 Act the 'reformers' began briskly by selling off the Corporation's wine, but the town only got a sewerage system in 1868.

Information about Russell's time in South Molton comes mainly from two sources: a diary that he began in September 1823 and kept intermittently until the 1830s and the South Molton parish registers. The evidence from the latter shows that from September 1823 to March 1825, the period of the first volume of his diary, Russell took 106 out of the parish's 158 baptisms, 126 out of 167 funerals and 55 out of 74 weddings. This works out at about ten duties a month over and above the two Sunday services, both with sermons, which Toms had declared as the norm when he had replied to Bishop Cary's queries in 1821.

The evidence from both registers and diaries shows the young clergyman to have been a more or less punctilious performer of the offices of the Church. Between September 1st 1823 and March 25th 1826, when he gave up the curacy of South Molton, Russell spent every Sunday 'Domi' as he put it. On six Sundays he left some time in the afternoon to go and stay with friends. On six other Sundays he did duty elsewhere, at Tiverton, Cheriton Fitzpaine, Winkleigh and twice at Iddesleigh covering for his brother William, who was their father's curate there. On the sixth occasion he did duty at both Romansleigh and Mariansleigh. Only one Sunday did he take completely off, April 17th, 1825 when he departed on a tour of Midland hunting establishments.

But this performance of routine duty was the sum of Russell's role as a clergyman of the Church of England, as it probably had been for his father and grandfather before him. The Easter weeks of 1824 and 1825 may show him at his best:
'Monday [April 12th,1824] Domi in the morning – dined at Bishop's Nympton, Court Day.
Tuesday. Domi in the morning, killed an otter in the marsh above Allen's lime pits in the afternoon.
Wednesday. Domi all day.
Thursday. Domi in the morning (a funeral). Killed an otter under White House below Pilcock wood in the afternoon.
Friday. Good Friday. Dom. (Two funerals and a baptism).
Saturday. Domi all day.
Sunday. Domi.'

Easter Week 1825 merely has 'domi' entered from Palm Sunday to Easter Sunday and is the longest 'no hunting' period in the years covered by the diaries. Easter week 1826 is not so laudable:
'Monday [March 20th] Domi. Rode to King's Nympton and returned.

G. Sharland came and William Underhill bought home Flash from Landue. [Flash was a horse and Landue a house near Launceston belonging to Tom Phillips, a hunting friend.]

Tuesday. Took my cry consisting of all sorts and sizes to Eggesford, found a fox in Burrow Cleave, ran him 1hr 50 minutes when Mr Fellowes requested me to stop them – took out the Squire's hounds, found three foxes in Tennerleigh Brake, ran one quick to Eggesford and lost.

Wednesday. Domi. (A baptism and a funeral).

Thursday. Domi. Beale brought the hounds from C. Eales.

Friday. Domi. Good Friday. (3 baptisms).

Saturday. Lady Day. Found a stag in Head Wood, ran him to Padely Wood, back over the hill to Heale Wood, New Place, South Copse, Beere, Lightly Moor, Hannacott, Kentsery, Stock to Ricksy Week, down the water to Answere, broke out across the S. Molton to Exeter road to Alswere weir, where I stopped them running hard. Gave up the Curacy of South Molton.

Sunday. Went to Buckland Church for Mr Stawell.'

Perhaps he was just demob happy.

Other examples can be found to demonstrate Russell's limitations as a clergyman – at least by later standards.

'Wednesday [June 22nd , 1825]. Mat Worth and Anstey at Dreyford Bridge with the hounds, found an otter under Eggesford kennel, no death. Left the hounds at Eggesford, came home, a great fire in East Street.

Thursday. Returned to Eggesford, hunted a trail to Snidel's Marsh, found an otter and killed ditto.'

Assuming that he was informed of the fire while at Eggesford it is something that he allowed it to interfere with his movements, though it cannot be determined with any certainty whether he returned out of a sense of pastoral duty or because the fire was near his home or for some other unknown reason. How differently one of the lions of the Evangelical Movement might have reacted to that 'great fire', which destroyed twelve houses and all their contents in East St – no doubt a great loss to a considerable number of his parishioners.

Another example of duty interrupting his pleasure only momentarily comes from September 1825 and is by no means untypical.

'Wednesday [14th]. Domi in the morning, went to Cruwys Morchard in the afternoon.

Thursday. Killed four hares.

Friday. Came home for Mrs Bryan's funeral, returned to Cruwys Morchard and dined there.'

This was a round trip of 30 miles and the evidence from his diaries is that he can have had little or no time for the pastoral care of his parishioners. Only twice in two and a half years does he reveal touches of the human reality of clerical life and both of these are social rather than pastoral.

'Wednesday [December 24th, 1823]. Hunted with Joe Bawden on Whitechapple and killed a brace of hares, dined with Jack Sanger, came home at two in the morning when the singers were tuning their pipes. Gave them grog and beer.

Thursday. Xmas day, domi.

Friday. Went to Barton and bought Kilbeck, Revel and Twister of Cooke, went to the Tiverton Ball in the evening from New Place [Chulmleigh], slept at New Place and came here next morning. Saw Froude's, Comin's and Worth's hounds in my way to Tiverton.'

Certainly a punishing routine, not one centred on the mystery of the Incarnation. He spent Christmas Eve in 1824 travelling to King's Brompton 'about the curacy', but it came to nothing.

The second hint of clerical life was on Tuesday, January 27th, 1824. 'Went with my brother Michael on Great Heale to give Sultan a course, but did not find a timid. Returned at two o'clock and dined with the Choristers at the Market House-Great Fun.' But otherwise there is nothing. It is only when a funeral such as Mrs Bryan's, a baptism or a wedding interrupted hunting that a reader of the diary might guess that the 'domi' on Sundays denoted the clergyman.

Some diarists like Kilvert are compulsive recorders of their thoughts and impressions, but one must wonder why Russell kept his. It is more than just a hunting diary, but less than a record of his life. One can discover, just, at whose board he dined and under whose roof he slept, but little more and never what he talked about and the only thoughts he recorded were satisfaction at the day's hunting or criticism of other people's hounds. 'Thursday [Feb 26th,1824] Met Mr Glub's hounds at Beaford Bridge, found a fox at Wanham but there being no devil in master or hounds I left them and went home to South Molton ...' 'Saturday. [May 22nd, 1824] Returned home and looked at Mr Freke's hounds – 14 pennyworth of dogs!!!' Queen Victoria did not have a monopoly of punctuation. His diaries tell of a crush on some girls at Washfield and they outline the course of his wooing of his future wife without ever telling us the colour of her hair, the shape of her nose, the chime of her voice or indeed anything about her except her name. These bare bones of a diary, which often dwindle to a scanty record of a day's sport reveal the limitations of the young Russell, a nice chap, a clubbable fellow, a man of great physical endurance, but a man who can keep a dairy from September 1823 to June 1826, from September 1827 to April 1828 and from August 1831 to May 1832 without a single comment on the stirring events of those times, many of vital importance to the Church of England: the Repeal of the Test and Corporation Acts, the Catholic Relief Act and the Reform Bill. Perhaps Russell was the only diarist writing in 1832 who did not mention the Reform Bill. Once there was a comment that his father was angry, another time regret at the injury to a horse. As time went on the entries confine themselves more and more to hunting, and this is fitting because Russell's fame was based on the development of a great talent for handling hounds, a deep understanding of the wiles of their quarry and a single minded interest in developing and enjoying those abilities, which he was able to do on a scale to achieve that fame because he married a rich wife. The same public taste that made Surtees a best seller puffed Russell first into local, then into national notoriety. He became a Jorrocks of real life with the additional spice of being a clergyman, who, thanks to a long life and an extraordinarily vigorous old age, hunted long after such activity was normal either for a layman or a clergyman. Grand Old Men are cherished out of a sense of nostalgia. Palmerston carried into the 1860s the manners and appearance of his Regency youth; similarly Russell became a period cameo, the fox-hunting squarson, an honest example of the unreformed eighteenth century Church of England, free of the ungentlemanly zeal of the Evangelicals and of the perfervidity of the Oxford Movement. He came to personify the old pre-industrial England, a part of that love of anachronism that still puts stage coaches on Christmas cards and which still sees hunting and the pink coat as an important part of rural life.

In the 1820s as curate of South Molton Russell was learning his craft. All accounts agree that he began his apprenticeship by keeping a 'cry' of otter hounds, as this was what he could afford on his stipend of £100 a year and a grant of £800 in 1820 from his grandfather Tyrell's money, probably occasioned by his mother's death. Davies wrote that Russell kept this 'cry' for six years and his diary shows that he last chased otter on May 22nd 1826, so perhaps the £800 was used to start up. The pack was spectacularly unsuccessful until Russell acquired a hound called 'Racer' from a Hatherleigh farmer, who in turn had got him from John Woolcombe of Ashbury. Racer was the key to the immediate killing of 35 otters. 'Nimrod', the sporting journalist, reported in 1824 that Russell had killed 'the almost incredible number of 25 otters in the last two summers, for which he must receive the thanks of the fish'.

Some of this can be substantiated. Racer did exist and was a knowledgeable and trusted hound: 'Friday [July 16th,1824] W. Ashford came to Baron's Down (nr Dulverton) with his hounds. They mark'd something in the Lower Barlinch Meadow which W.A. pronounced to be a bubble, notwithstanding my opinion to the contrary, as my hounds took but little notice of the scent. We dug and it turned out to be a rabbit – we hit a trail and went up to Kent's with the scent and found him, but the water suddenly became very dirty and we lost him.

Saturday. Took trail at Kent's and Racer found the otter just below Winsford, but happening to turn up the Quarme with the other hounds [I] did not know it. Afterwards took the hounds to where Racer had been marking, but could not hunt him. Returned domi.'

Russell met 'Nimrod', *nom de plume* of Charles Appesley, on September 21st, 1824. He renewed the acquaintance the following Friday: 'Met the Stag Hounds at Bray Cross, found a stag at Popham Wood and killed him after a poor run at Bray Ford, dined with Lewes, met Nimrod and Michael.

Saturday. Went with Nimrod to Baron's Down, shew'd ditto the Lions [?], dined at Anstey and returned domi.

Sunday. Domi.

Monday. Rode the Tailor to Exeter in three hours. Took Fanny from thence, accompanied by Nimrod and Lewis and rode to Chudleigh Rock to meet Templer, found a varmint at Bellamarsh, no scent, turned down two bagmen, took up the same and dined at Ashill.

Tuesday. Showed Nimrod the Lions [?] at Ashill in the morn; dined at Exeter with Michael, Baillie, Lewes and Nimrod and slept there.'

This companionship was obviously the source of Nimrod's information about the killing of those 25 otters. Before his entry of September 1st, 1823 Russell wrote 'Previous to Sept 1st I killed in the summer of that season 11 otters with my own hounds.' In the summer of 1824 his diary reveals the killing of a further 15 and to kill these 15 he went otter hunting 74 times. The 'cry's' most successful day was 'Wednesday. [September 1st, 1824] Took the Bubbles to Chulmleigh and tried the Dart and Taw, had a beautiful trail from Chulmleigh Clapper, the hounds went heel up to Chawleigh Cleaves where a fox went away in view from an aller bed which the hounds were trying, they were stopped and taken down to the water. They hit the trail across some fields to the Taw where they marked, and drew out two young otters, a third we saved and brought home. He lived till Sunday following and died.'

In these six years as Master of Otterhounds, if this is not too grandiose a description of the assorted dogs that made up his 'cry', Russell travelled up and down all the river valleys of central Devon. Between April and December 1824, for example, he not only hunted the Bray, Mole, Taw and Little Dart on his doorstep, but he also ranged the Barle, Sheardown and Exe as far south as Cowley Bridge and sought the 'bubble' on the smaller rivers of the north coast, the Heddon, the East and West Lyn and the waters of Williton, Watchet, Porlock, Timberscombe and Stogumber. He also sampled the Creedy, Torridge, Bovey Teign and Ventifer and in these years laid the basis of an intimate knowledge of the Devon countryside. One must agree with Davies that 'his long tramps in quest of the otter did not prove altogether profitless, for then he acquired that rare knowledge of his country, which ever since has remained, like an Ordnance Map, imprinted in his memory. In after years, on many a starless night, with many a mile between him and his kennels, through ravines dark as Erebus, through fords flooded by storms, over the pathless moor, by bog, fell and precipice, that knowledge did him good service, bringing him always, like an instinct of a carrier pigeon, safely to his home.' One can only assume that, in his own way, Russell was influenced by the beauty of the Devon countryside and the passing pageant of the seasons, as there are no entries in the diaries that give the slenderest hint that huntsman, hounds, moor, river and woods were ever folded into a Wordsworthian whole.

This period of otter hunting was also important in teaching Russell how to handle hounds. Hounds naturally will chase deer, hare and fox and, unaided, will kill, but they need to be taught how to chase otter and, unaided and uncontrolled, will find it almost impossible to kill. Otter hunting may not produce the blood stirring cross-country runs of stag and fox hunting, but it needs a more sophisticated partnership of man and hound. This skill with hounds Russell probably possessed intuitively, but he developed it to a greater pitch as an 'M.O.H.' of an effective, if quaintly heterogeneous pack.

Otter were not his only quarry. As 'Nimrod' wrote: 'There is another gent, the Rev. John Russell, but much better known by the name of Jack Russell, who stands high among the Devonshire bruisers. This gent finds hunting so conducive to his health that with stag hounds, fox hounds, harriers and otter hounds he contrives to enjoy it all the year round.' The introductory entry to his diary, besides mentioning the killing of 11 otter, continues, 'beside a great number of flitches [wild cats] I was in at the death of —— deer'. Between 1818 and 1824 the Stag Hounds were managed by Stucley Tristram Lucas of Baron's Down in Brompton Regis, whose son, another Stucley had left Blundell's School a little before Russell's arrival. Every Tuesday in September 1823, as well as two Fridays and a Saturday, Russell hunted with the Stag

Hounds, usually staying at Baron's Down to do so. In 1824 he hunted with them on most Tuesdays and every Friday in April and May. The Tuesday-Friday pattern was repeated in the autumn, the diary giving an especially full account on September 3rd: 'Went with Riccard to meet the Stag Hounds at Hawkridge, they had moved on to Burrow Wood, we followed them, they found a stag which came out in view of 100 horsemen on Winsford Hill, which he crossed to Bradley, Withypool, Lanacre Bridge, Sheardown Hutch, Cow Castle, Newland, Exe Cleave, Alderman's Burrow where he stood still and allowed the hounds to come up to him. We were nearly an hour taking him, six only were up, viz J. Jenkins, Ld H Kerr, Mr Chorley of the Quorn, Riccard, old John Caldicott aged seventy-four on 'Random' and myself on 'Fanny' – a most brilliant day's sport.' Such a large field was not unusual; a few weeks later on September 21st Russell estimated that 500 were out, perhaps stimulated by the presence of 'Nimrod'. However stag hunting fades out of Russell's diary at the end of the autumn season of 1824, which accords with the known history of the Hunt, for, after Mr Lucas gave up the Mastership, no-one else was prepared to take it on and the hounds were sold to a German Baron. Stag hunting was only restarted on a regular basis in 1841 when the Hon. Newton Fellowes became Master. Between 1824 and 1841 the red deer of Exmoor were decimated by poachers.

From October to March Russell hunted hares, or, as he called them, 'timids'. Between November 1st, 1823 and February 29th 1824 he was out after hare on 38 occasions, besides shooting on a further twenty-one days and fox hunting on sixteen, that is he hunted on seventy-five out of ninety days. More often than not his companion when hunting hare was the Rev. John Froude of Knowstone, 'Friday [February 16th, 1824] Hunted with Froude at Nutcombe, killed one hare – very good sport. Riccard and Michael out, the latter on 'Linchpin'.
Saturday. Domi all day.
Sunday. Michael went to Iddesleigh.
Monday. Met Froude at Sidemoor, he was running a hare, fresh found her and after taking a turn round Baples, Moortown woods etc she went straight across Ash Moor and was killed at Irishcombe. Found a second at Irishcombe and chopped her. Found a third which ran a beautiful country round the Witheridge Moors and was killed after an hour and thirty five minutes of the best hunting and racing I ever witnessed, in a field adjoining the south side of Ash Moor. N.B. The best day's sport I have seen this season.
Tuesday. Rode with Froude to see Mr Karslake's hounds and Mr Hole's [of Eberly] hounds – returned domi to dinner, went to the Ball and Froude decamped'. The next Friday he also hunted hare with Froude.

It is quite clear even from this short extract that Russell's relationship with Froude was close. In the last four months of 1823 he spent eighteen days wholly or partly in Froude's company, and in 1824 thirty-two days in his company. Many are the stories of the wicked parson Jack of Knowstone and into many of them is woven the name of Jack Russell. Perhaps the best known of them is the one that tells of them brawling in a muddy lane after a row in the hunting field when Russell had remonstrated with Froude about his bad language. All accounts have someone breaking up the fight by mentioning Bishop Phillpotts and the possibility of the affair getting into the Radical papers. So if the incident ever happened it cannot have been before Phillpotts became Bishop of Exeter when Russell would have been thirty-seven and Froude fifty-four.

Davies omitted this tale, but told of Russell spending his first Oxford exhibition money buying a horse from Froude and getting a very bad bargain. Yet a few pages later Davies tells us the same horse was bought from a dealer named Rookes. Sabine-Gould takes the tale further by telling of a time when Russell tried to get Froude drunk to sell him a horse with cataracts, a plot the wily Froude easily foiled. Other Froude stories have as little a basis in reality. One told by Davies was of a visit by Phillpotts to Knowstone Rectory to follow up some complaints. The Bishop found Froude wrapped up and seemingly ill, pretending to be too deaf to hear a word, and in mock hospitality pressing copious brandy on the abstemious prelate. But Davies then has Russell correct the story as follows. Froude, having been apprised of the Bishop's coming, retired to bed. Jane, his housekeeper , ushered Phillpotts into the parlour, saying that Froude was in bed with a fever.

'Nothing serious, I hope', said the Bishop. 'I dare say he would not object to see me at his bedside'.

'Perhaps not, my Lord,' Jane hesitantly replied. 'Leastwise, if you bean't afeered o' going there. 'Tis a faver o' some soart, but I can't mind what the doctor call'th it.'

'A fever did you say? Rheumatic, perhaps, from exposure to the wet?'

'No, no; I've got that myself bad enough. 'Tis something a great deal worse I reckon.'

'Not scarlet fever, I hope?'

The housekeeper shook her head. 'Worse than that, my Lord.'

'Typhus?' inquired the Bishop with alarm

'Iss, that's it; seem'th to me that's what the doctor ca'd it.' Upon which Phillpotts picked up his hat and drove off smartest and Froude got up and went off hunting.

There is corroboration of this version in Phillpotts' own diary. On July 19th, 1831 he wrote: 'Went to Knowstone – Mr Froude ill in bed – the

Church good – house fair – in dining-room 6 fox brushes – two of bell pulls with a fox engraved – and "tally-ho" upon them. He wished to see me – message through Mr Hodgkin my companion. Mr Stranger, the curate, seems an estimable young man, much liked at Knowstone and Molland.'

Russell told Davies that Froude hunted three days a week and shot on the others, that he was witty and original and what the dull, slow thinkers of to-day might stigmatise as a 'loose cannon'. Froude has had a bad press, but the joy of the man is that he would not have cared a damn.

The energy that Russell expended shooting, stag hunting and chasing otter would have exhausted most men. But fox-hunting was the real love of his life and he had already experienced its delights with the crack Midland establishments, like the Heythrop, while at Oxford. His fox hunting career between coming down from Oxford in 1819 and the beginning of his diary in September 1823 will probably always be a blank, but during the winter of 1823-4 he hunted fox on 25 occasions. Sometimes he used his own mixed cry, at other times he combined them with the hounds of his friend and fellow Old Blundellian, Joshua Bawden, a member of a large South Molton family, whose main interest was banking. The first fox killed by this mixed pack was found on October 17th, 1823. 'Hunting with Jo Bawden, found a fox at Rowley [in Romansleigh] and killed him after a 7 mile run at Cove Bridge. Hole, Riccard and Jo Bawden in at the death. I have the brush'.

In the same winter Russell had hunted foxes on several occasions with Newton Fellowes of Eggesford and Dr Troyte of Huntsham. While they had found plenty of foxes none had been killed and one senses Russell's frustration as he probably thought he could do better. On December 1st, 1823 he had his chance: 'Hunted with Froude on Kerscott [5 miles east of South Molton] found a hare and lost the same immediately, tried a long while and found another on Week which was chopped. After trying some time longer Froude went home having company to dinner and left the hounds with me, and in drawing Harpson Brake they found a fox, he went to Baples Wood and turned short back through Harpson Wood to Honeycleave Wood, Rose Ash, Bishop's Nympton, through Hayne Plantation, Broadhill, Week, Woolland, Kimmins, Honeycleave Wood, Ash Moor, Nethercott Plantation, Yarde Wood, Quince Brake and to Nethercott Plantation again. They viewed him into the plantation and from the appearance of the hounds next day it is most likely they killed him. They found at half past three o'clock and killed him at seven, a very brilliant run, particularly the first hour and a quarter when he was coursed by a sheep dog and the scent altered very much for the worse. I returned home and found William Ward, Cutcliffe and Michael taking their beakers, having dined.' By the length of time taken and the meticulousness of the map reading it is probable that Froude's pack hunted slowly and carefully with their noses and were still no faster than the average 'Goose and Dumpling' pack. But there is such an air of pride and self-satisfaction in the account that one wonders if this may have been his first 'kill' as a huntsman in charge of hounds.

On December 29th he was out with Froude's hounds again. 'Monday. Hunted with Froude – found a fox in Hayne Plantation, he went away with every hound at him to Veraby where J. Bawden's hounds viewed him. I took off Froude's – Joe's earth'd him at Kingswood, returned to Hayne and found several more foxes, one went away to Park, Ward Mill water where we believe he was drowned, as we could not find him from the river above Ward Mill.' It seems clear that Russell was working the hounds and had persuaded Froude to try for foxes. One cannot take too many imaginative leaps on the basis of this thin material, but, perhaps more confident of his skill, Russell is pushing himself forward. Certainly there is now a strong strain of impatience in his description of poor performance. 'Jan 17th, 1824. Hunted with Joe Bawden on Blastridge, but the hounds having divided and behaved as usual very ill, I returned home and dined with the Corporation'. On February 26th he slated the Rev. P. Glubb, the Rector of Torrington, 'There being no devil in Master or hounds I went home'. In May Mr Freke of South Tawton's cry is condemned as '14 pennyworth of dogs'.

This impatience even comes out in his description of hunting with Newton Fellowes, the great Squire of Eggesford, a man who stood very high in his own estimation and the ruins of whose great castellated mansion brood on the hills above Eggesford Station. In the 1823-4 season Russell hunted nine times with Fellowes' hounds, but they killed only once, on March 18th. On January 3rd, 'ran a fox and lost him'; on the 18th 'found a fox but could do nothing'; on February 21st 'found a fox but could not get him away'; on March 17th 'found Charley immediately, ran him and lost him'. Even the kill on March 18th was uninteresting, 'Mat Mr Fellowes on Labdon, had a tolerable run and killed our fox at Howard'.

Russell still hunted with Fellowes in the 1824-5 season, but for a time the sport remained very limited. On November 2nd they 'ran him to Romansleigh and lost him'; on the 16th they 'ran him and lost ditto'. Friday December 10th was even sadder: 'Met Mr Fellowes at West Yeo,

*Sandhill, Calstock where Russell spent his earlier years, just
down the hill from his maternal grandfather's place at Dimson.*
(By permission of the present owners)

*Old Blundell's. The Green was the grass in front of the School, and the Ironing Box
the triangle in front of the buildings where fights took place. This print dates from
the 1840s and they would not have been playing cricket in Russell's time.*

South Molton church to which Russell came as a curate until his marriage in 1826. His sister Nora, until her early death lived within yards of where this view was taken and his brother-in-law, Riccard lived there until his death. (DRO)

The Bury's house, Dennington, in Swimbridge. The Admiral must have died in his carriage accident near here in 1825. (Taken by A.C.D. Noon)

Castle Hill, Filleigh, the home of Earl Fortescue. This house, which Russell knew, was destroyed by a fire in the 1930s and was subsequently restored to its original proportions. It was the home of the Viscount Ebrington for whom Admiral Bury canvassed and whom Russell's father opposed in the election of 1818. (DRO)

St James', Iddesleigh, where Russell
was his father's curate from 1826-33.
A delightful village with a delightful
church and this view is taken from the
direction of its delightful pub.
(The Beaford Archive)

Hayne House, Stowford, the mansion of Christopher Arthur Mohun Harris, Russell's hunting partner of the Iddesleigh years. The Harris family were connected with the Walpoles, from whom they may have acquired the taste for Gothick. (DRO)

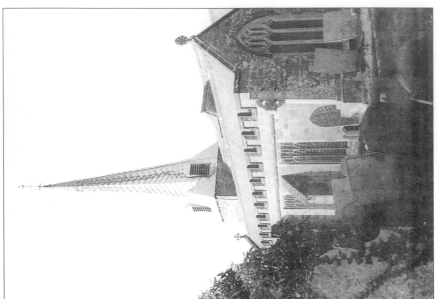

St James', Swinbridge, where Russell served from 1833-79. A view taken from near Penelope and John Russell's grave. (Taken by A.C.D. Noon)

The still standing entrance to St Hubert's Hall, the folly Christopher Harris created from an old quarry for the delectation of his hunting friends, in the private grounds of Hayne House. (Taken by S. Goodwin)

Eggesford House, built by Newton Fellowes in the 1830s
in the latest and most fashionable style. (DRO)

Colleton Barton, the house near Chulmleigh which Russell inherited from Admiral and
Mrs Bury and which he sold in the 1850s to pay off some debts. (Taken by A.C.D. Noon)

Sir Walter Palk Carew en famille *and wearing the black hat.*
The man who wished to set his dogs on the agents of Bishop Phillpotts
if they came poking around in 'his' parish. His heart must have been
in the right place. (Lent by Sir Rivers Carew)

Sir Walter Carew's yacht, the Evadne, *the successor to the one*
Russell reluctantly sailed in. (Lent by Sir Rivers Carew)

drew Ashbeer Plantation when Carew's hounds brought a fox into the mouths of the hounds, they ran him very sharp to Irishcombe Plantation and changed to a fresh fox, which went to Hayne. He broke away again and we lost him at Marley'. But after Christmas there was an improvement in the performance of Fellowes' pack. Either someone else was hunting them, or better hounds had been drafted in, or, as I suspect, George Templer had affected the conduct of affairs. Whatever the cause the run on January 15th, 1825 is typical of the new performance, 'Met Mr Fellowes at Allswear, found a fox on Romansleigh Parsonage, and killed ditto after a pretty run of 1 hour and fifty minutes at Irishcombe.'

As far as the evidence from his diary goes Russell's initial meeting with George Templer of Stover House had been inauspicious. in October 1823 he had spent an unsuccessful week hunting with Templer's pack. In May 1824 he had taken his otter hounds to Stover and had returned in June to play cricket at Teignbridge. In early July he had spent a week with J. Lyne Templer, going to the Totnes races and ending up at Stover as a member of a house party that included his two brothers, William and Michael. By this time the friendship was close enough for George Templer to get hold of Russell's diary on October 6th, 1824 and to make an extravagantly lewd entry: 'Woke with a fit of the Horn Colic – sent for my woman – but found it was the Chamber pot I wanted and looked very foolish.' In his own hand Russell then wrote: 'N.B. The above is an effusion of George Templer Esq.' and he then went on with a routine entry.

Probably Russell's acquaintance with George Templer dated from Blundell's or Exeter College days. Three of George's brothers were sent to Blundell's, though the last, John Templer, left aged sixteen four years before Russell's arrival. A John Templer of Exeter College was in the same group taking Responsions and the same John Templer took his degree a few months before Russell. Such may have been the means of Russell's entry to Stover, the Templer mansion overlooking the Teign, built from the profits made by George's father, James Templer, from the Haytor Quarries. To facilitate the marketing of the granite James Templer dug the Stover Canal to Ventiford between 1790 and 1792 and George expanded the business and in 1820 began to construct a unique tramway with rails of granite to a gauge of 4 foot 3 inches from Haytor to Ventiford. This Haytor granite was used to build London Bridge, the British Museum and the National Gallery. When Russell first began to visit Stover the house must have been at its grandest and most opulent. But the goings-on in the elegant house may hardly have been a suitable preparation for its present use as a girls' school.

Its owner was certainly an interesting character and a key figure in the early history of fox hunting in Devon. C.A. Harris, who also experienced Stover in the early 1820s, later wrote, 'To enlarge upon his several excellencies, his amiability, the sincerity of his friendship and benevolence of disposition adorned by a graceful erudition and enlivened by a playful wit that made him the charm of society, is but to repeat an oft told tale. The epoch of George Templer of Stover, on many accounts and for many a long year will be the *alba nota* in the sporting annals of Devonshire, for there was a graceful individuality that belonged to the man, that made him remarkable at any time'. [*Letters on the Past and Present Foxhounds of Devonshire*, 1861.] Templer had been a 'Meltonian' and had introduced the new style of fox hunting to his native county, but with some eccentric embellishments. When Russell had showed 'Nimrod' round Templer's kennels, the great man must have been astonished by what he was told as well as by what he saw. In his *Hunting Tours* 'Nimrod' wrote that he had witnessed the Stover party trick of releasing a bagged fox in front of the hounds. While the hounds stayed put, no doubt squirming with excitement, the bagman was given five minutes grace before the hounds were urged on its trail. Russell later added that one sharp hound did not even look at the fox, but kept its gaze fixed on whoever was holding the stopwatch, awaiting the signal. These bagmen were not killed, but taken up alive in front of the hounds. Tradition has it, and 'Nimrod' confirmed it, that this feat was performed by the Whips, who usually were the Reverends Henry Taylor of Ogwell and Jack Russell of South Molton. 'Nimrod, also reported that one fox, called 'The Bold Dragoon' had been put down to hounds 36 times. Another fox would wag its tail when it recognised a visitor and 'Nimrod' also reported the presence of a jackal.

Some stories, not related by 'Nimrod' have been handed down by Templer's descendants via C.A. Harris, and bizarre they are – of a monkey hunting strapped to a horse and rabbits hunted by packs of foxes or by mixed packs of foxes and terriers. In later days Russell never stinted his praise of Templer's abilities as Master. In 1863 in a letter to C.A Harris he wrote, 'I think the Duke of Beaufort is the best sportsman I ever knew. I say "I think" because during poor, dear George Templer's lifetime I was not, – could not be, as good a judge as I may be at present. The latter was the best man over a country, and even in Devonshire saw every turn hounds made,' Froude and Templer were Russell's mentors.

But George Templer was more than an able and idiosyncratic sportsman. It is obvious he possessed that something, which cannot be fully grasped at this distance, that lifts a man into memorability. His hospitality at Stover was lavish in those days before the railway when

Devonian society was truly provincial with all the clannish virtues and vices that phrase implies. The host preserved some of the spirit of those house parties in verse – for instance 'A Party at Stover' allegedly written in 1823, perhaps during that week in October when Russell was a visitor. It is reproduced in Appendix 2.

After his life had been steeled by financial disaster, some of Templer's verses become less ephemeral. In 1825 the crash came due to a combination of a way of life grander than resources really allowed, to business over-extension and, as Templer himself averred in some very bitter verse, to the activities of a dishonest attorney. The result was the sale of Stover, the granite business and the Canal and he lived out the rest of his life in reduced circumstances at Sandford Orleigh, still hunting, but with other people's hounds. The crash produced 'Farewell to Stover'.

> Stover farewell! Still fancy's hand shall trace
> Thy pleasure's past in all their former grace,
> And I will wear and cherish, though we part,
> Thy dear remembrance ever at my heart.
>
> Not as the hare, whom horn and hounds pursue,
> In timid constancy I cling to you,
> But, like some bolder chase, resolved I fly
> That, where I may not live, I will not die.
>
> And now Remorse! with thee prepared to go,
> These scenes I leave for wider fields of woe,
> On foreign shores unheeded scenes I shed
> For bygone bliss and brighter moments fled.

His most famous poem was originally declaimed at a dinner of the Chulmleigh Club, an annual focus of Devon fox hunting in the 1810s and 1820s. In his *Sporting Tour* Nimrod reported on the doings of the Club and included the gastronomic snippet that 'as proof of the force of local customs at these dinners there was a course of plum pudding and tongue eaten together'. When Nimrod was there the Club Week consisted of hunting on alternate days with Newton Fellowes', and Sir Arthur Chichester's packs, which were followed by the 'principal gents of the country'. The poem was entitled ' Farewell to My Horn'.

> Though toil has somewhat worn my frame
> And time hath marred thy beauty
> Come forth lone relic of my fame
> Thou well hast done thy duty

Time was when other tongues would praise
Thy wavering notes of pleasure
Now, miserlike, alone I gaze
On thee, a worthless treasure.

Some hearts may prize thy music still,
But ah! how changed thy story,
Since first Devonia felt the thrill
That roused her sporting glory.

Grace still in every vale abounds,
But one dear charm is wanting,
No more I hear thy gallant hounds
In chorus blithely chaunting.

And there my steed has found a rest
Beneath the mountain heather
That oft, like comrades sworn, we've pressed
In pleasure's train together.

And some, who at thy call would wake,
Hath friendship long been weeping
A shriller note than thine must break
Their deep and dreamless sleeping.

I too the fading wreath resign
For friends and fame are fleeting
Around this bolder brow to twine
Where younger blood is beating.

Henceforth be mute my trusted horn
Since time hath marred thy beauty,
And I, like thee, by toil am worn -
We both hath done our duty.

This elicited a reply from Paul Treby, the subject of the fourth verse of 'The Party at Stover', whose nickname in the fraternity was 'Byron the Second'.

'Twas when I heard thy parting song,
And sad yet sweet adieu,
A rush of feeling drove along
And brought the past to view.

Methought I heard the horn's sweet sound,
And the melodious voice,
Which sweetly cheered the leading hound
And bade us all rejoice

Methought I saw the brilliant smile
Flit o'er the sunny face,
Which oft thy comrades did beguile
Thy comrades of the chase.

Alas 'twas but a pleasant thought,
A vision of the day,
By nights of melancholy wrought,
The joys have passed away.

Enough! No muse's aid I seek
To greet thee ere we part,
For me the trickling tear must speak,
For me, the throbbing heart.

Russell refers to a 'Club Week' beginning on October 12th, 1824, just after 'Nimrod' had left the county. 'Met Sir Arthur's hounds at Burrow Moor Gate, found a fox after trying several hours in Bycott Plantation, he went away but they did nothing with him. Chulmleigh Club Week – Ball Night.

Wednesday. Domi in the morning. Shot on Hacche with Michael – no sport – had four shots at a woodcock – missed every time.

Thursday. Met at Brayly Bridge with the cry, found a fox at Huxtable, ran him for an hour and fifty minutes with only one check and killed him in Gratton Wood. Templer took the hounds to Chulmleigh. I went with him and dined at the Club and slept at B. Radford's [the Rector of Lapford].'

Club Weeks follow in February and March 1825 and again in November. This November 'Week' was very active indeed. From November 23rd to December 7th Russell hunted on twelve consecutive days barring the Sundays.

'Wednesday November 23rd. Had a long day in the Lapford country – no death, dined and slept at New Place [the Chulmleigh home of the Bullers].

Thursday. Bad day [usually a phrase he used to refer to the hunting], dined at Cockerham, Chicken Pye Club at Mr Bawden's, very jolly.

Friday. With Mr Fellowes in the Lapford covers – at three o'clock a fox went away to Kennerleigh, but ran us out of scent at Morchard at half past five. Slept at New Place.

Saturday. Found a fox at Cooke's Meadow – earthed him at Chawley Week, bolted him thro' Cleeves etc to Tunnivele Wood and changed.

Sunday. Domi.

Monday. Found a fox with Mr Fellowes at Irishcombe Plantation, a beautiful run to the Lapford covers and changed. First day of the Club.

Tuesday. Met at Bycott. No sport.

Wednesday. Found at Hayne, killed at Quince Brake.

Thursday. Dec 1st. Found a fox with the little cry at Wixon Plantation, ran him a complete burst to Satterleigh, chang'd and lost.

Friday. Mr F. found in Padeleigh Wood – a good run to Leyland Wood and changed.

Saturday. Found a fox in stone Wood, killed in Nott's Wood.

Sunday. Domi.

Monday. At Lapford Forches – found at Broadhay – bad weather – no death.

Tuesday. At Torrington, found at Potheridge, took alive in the town at 6 o'clock.

Wednesday. Found at Hayne, lost at China [sic].

Thursday. Domi all day.'

Friday and Saturday were spent hunting at Chittlehamholt and North Molton and every day of the following week Russell also spent hunting.

This was the last season Russell spent as a bachelor. In spite of his youth and the shortness of his purse – 'tightness of the chest' was his pet phrase for it, he was clearly one of Devon's foremost sportsmen, worthy of a paragraph to himself from 'Nimrod'. 'There is another of the same cloth, the Rev. John Russell, but much better known by the name of Jack Russell, who hunts a great deal with Mr Templer, and who also stands high among the Devonshire bruisers. This gent finds hunting so conducive to his health that with stag hounds, fox hounds, harriers and otter hounds he contrives to enjoy it all the year round'.

When Templer went to London to try to repair his shaken affairs, Russell hunted his hounds around Eggesford and on January 26th summed up his achievements: 'Templer came home from London after an absence of six weeks – during which I killed eight foxes and earthed the ninth'. Sadly Templer had to sell his hounds, most of them going to Yeatman of Stock House, Sherborne, another clerical Old Blundellian. Unaided Russell would never have had the resources to collect another pack of fox hounds, and only marriage would provide the wealth for Russell to avoid being a clerical Jack Sproggan to another Earl of Scamperdale.

One way Russell may have taken to overcome his congenital 'tightness of chest' was horse dealing. He knew his way round the local racecourses and in 1824 attended the Totnes, Tiverton and Haldon Races. 'Thursday [July 8th, 1824,] Rode to Totnes Races, saw the fun and returned to dinner. Prandium bene. Bought 'Broadby' of J. Lyne Templer.' A few days earlier he had 'tried Bullen's horse for Elton, wrote ditto.' So it is not altogether surprising that he was entrusted with the sale of Templer's horses after the crash.

This interest in horse trading may explain his presence at Exeter Assizes on July 26th and 27th, 1825. The *Exeter Flying Post* reported those days' cases and unhappy reading they make. For George Davies, aged sixteen, charged with burglary, but not actually stealing anything, just caught in the act, the death penalty; for Thomas Collacott for stealing four watches at Great Torrington, the death penalty; for Thomas Friendship, who 'received' one of them, fourteen years' transportation. The case that probably interested Russell was the trial of Henry Perceval, who was charged with stealing a horse. He had hired it from The White Hart in Exeter and disappeared with it, but had been traced to South Molton by evidence from the toll gate keepers. He was found in bed at The George Inn, having sold the horse to Fry a South Molton horse dealer for seven guineas. The *Flying Post* continued: 'The Judge immediately proceeded to pass sentence, and in addressing the prisoner observed he was exceedingly sorry to see him placed in this situation and convicted on the clearest evidence of an offence of late so frequent and for which the utmost rigour of the law had been withheld for some years. The prevalence of this crime rendered it necessary that punishment of death should again be resorted to in order to check, if possible, its alarming progress. He could hold out little hope to the prisoner that his life would be spared. In passing the awful sentence of the law it was impossible not to remember that he had been indicted for a similar offence and had probably escaped conviction by the absence of a material witness... He advised him not to foster delusive hopes of the Royal Clemency, but to attend to the advice of those friends who had taken so kind an interest in his fate and to prepare himself by repentance and prayer for that change it was possible he should soon undergo. He would not make any further observations as he perceived the anguish of mind by which he was oppressed, and it only remained for him to pass the awful sentence of law. This his lordship did in the usual form. The unhappy man, though he had seemed perfectly collected – while the jury were consulting he looked steadfastly towards the box – on hearing the verdict he leaned his head on the bar in dreadful agitation. He manifested the same intense anxiety amounting almost to inanition during the Judge's address and it was not until he was ordered to be removed that consciousness seemed to return, when in turning to go down he fainted and was borne off by the turnkeys. He was dressed in a new suit of black and his hair was turned aside, he was almost twenty-seven years old and 5 ft 5 inches in height, but there is NOT anything prepossessing in his person'.

The 1820s were tough and often brutal and there is much in Russell's diary that appals almost as much as those court scenes. On July 12th, 1824 he turned out a bagged otter into a flooded lime pit 'to amuse the ladies, but the nobility crowded round the pit so much he was soon killed'. The next day he turned out and killed a bagged badger. At Stover in March 1825 he took part in killing six bagged foxes to blood new hounds.

Apart from hunting and going to the Assizes he went to the theatre twice, at Tiverton and at Bath. He was a member of a Chicken Pye club, which was of sufficient importance that he made a special overnight journey from Jacobstowe to South Molton to attend it in December 1823. He also took part in the civic pomps and circumstances of that little town. In September 1823 he dined at the Town Hall off a haunch of venison. Every November 5th he dined with the Corporation to celebrate the national deliverance from Popish Tricks. Like his father he was a loyal Old Blundellian and regularly attended the Old Boys' feasts. In July 1824 he went to a tea party at the Cutcliffes and on his birthday, December 21st, he invited '17 lads to dine with him'. He attended Barnstaple Fair and Swimbridge Revel, but his diaries are dominated by hunting and are evidence of a full, yet limited life.

But they do allow a recreation of his courtship and marriage to Penelope Incledon Bury.

Chapter Five

LOVE AND MARRIAGE

Doubtless the mating urge has been a constant of History, but the conventions and rituals of courtship have undergone radical changes in the last twenty years and the gulf separating us from the 'Game of Love' as played in the 1820s is wide and deep. Not that the 1820s were uniform in this respect. Did the 'Stover Gang' incline to the wild world of Byron or the 'Chulmleigh Club' lean to the graded niceties of Jane Austen? There were no discos at Old Blundell's in Russell's day, with their groping explorations and heavy petting. No doubt a few of Russell's acquaintances at Oxford dabbled with ladies of the town and Denne obviously had a romance. Russell was handsome and sociable, and I do not think he was too concerned about the state of his own soul, so he may have had an undergraduate rite of passage during his Oxford years

But the naiveté of the diary entries where young women are concerned suggests the contrary. The diary is regularly punctuated with accounts of attendance at 'Balls'. He went to two balls in Tiverton in November 1823 and another on Boxing Day. In early 1824 he attended a further three balls in Tiverton and two in South Molton. Two further balls followed in Tiverton in August – the Blundellian Feast Ball on the 26th, and a ball connected with Tiverton races on the 27th. I defy any young man to go to ten balls and not get a crush on someone and Russell was no exception. In January 1824 his descriptions of hunting go out of their way to mention whenever Miss Turner and Miss Worth are out. The latter lived at Worth in Washfield parish only a mile from Tiverton and the former was obviously a friend of Miss Worth's, but it is impossible to tell which of the two he was interested in. But he was certainly interested: 'August 26th. Tiverton School Meeting. Went to the Ball etc, etc,!.' This excessive punctuation was followed by a dot surrounded by a circle, but meaning what? On August 27th he went to Tiverton races, galloped home for a Dr Bryan's funeral, rushed back to Tiverton for a ball and the evening races and then went home. The entry for Saturday 28th is merely '!!!!'

For the next fortnight the diary returns to its hunting normal, punctuated by only one social event, 'Saturday [September 4th] Dined with Froude's sisters and nieces'. But the week beginning Monday 13th September is more interesting: 'Walked into Tiverton and dined at Worth.

Tuesday. Met Stag Hounds at Huntsham, returned home on Worth's Woodlark.

Wednesday. Went to Lynmouth.

Thursday. Returned from Lynmouth and went to W......d in the eve.' This is unique in the whole diary as being a place name disguised, but it is obviously Washfield. He spent all of Friday and Saturday at 'W.....d'.

His constant companion in the next few weeks was George Templer and his constant occupation was hunting and showing 'Nimrod' the sights. It is at this point, on Wednesday 6th October that Templer wrote in Russell's diary: 'Woke with a fit of the Horn Colic, sent for my woman, but found it was the chamber pot I wanted and looked very foolish' One wonders if Russell had been talking of W....d and of the facts behind the exclamation marks. In the second half of October Russell returned to his W....d theme:

'Monday [October 18th] Hunted around South Molton in the morning and went to W....d in the afternoon.

Tuesday. Remained at W....d, rode out cum puellis to see Mr and Mrs Were [Tiverton residents].

Wednesday. Came home from W....d in the morning and dined with Mr Stawell.

Thursday. Returned to W.......d and dined there. Ah! miseranda dies puellis sed non mihi'.

After that Latin ejaculation there is not a single mention of 'W....d' nor of the puellae. In late October he mentions 'Sweet Kitty Clarence' and in early 1825 he refers to a 'Jenny' while dining with his brother-in-law, Riccard.

Then he met Penelope Incledon Bury. When an old man, Russell gave Otter Davies an edited version of the facts. 'Towards the end of 1825, or the beginning of 1826, an event affecting the happiness of Russell's life, at home and abroad, bid fair, at least for a time, to imperil the devotion, which, up to this period, he had so exclusively shown to the sylvan

Queen , who beyond all doubt had reigned in his heart without a rival.

'But strong and enduring as the bonds were in which the goddess retained her willing captive, the time had now arrived when they were destined to prove but as green withes compared with those of Venus, whose power both the gods and men have alike shown to be irresistible.

'About this time he met with a lady whose attractions at once arrested the current of his thoughts, and brought him on bended knee to sue for her hand. That lady was Miss Penelope Incledon Bury, the daughter of Admiral and Mrs Bury, of Dennington House, near Barnstaple. Both the father and mother being pure North Devoners, and claiming descent from two good old county families, they were proud of the 'haveage' to which they belonged. Nor could they have taken exception to Russell's pedigree; he himself being a descendant of the Russells of Kingston-Russell. [Readers of Chapter 1 will realise how true that statement might be.] Mrs Bury, the mother of Penelope, was of the knightly family of Chichester, of Hall.' Significantly Russell did not mention his own mother, from whose family what prosperity he possessed had been obtained, but the Terrells of Dimson had been very middle-class and the story that Russell gave Davies is edited.

Let us work backwards. On May 30th, 1826 Russell wrote 'Took Penelope Incledon Bury to wife, adjourned with ditto in a chariot and four, furnished by Pratt of Old London, Exeter, to South Molton and Tiverton and slept at the George Inn, Bridgwater.' Underneath he later wrote, 'Boy born 31st May 1827!! Xtened John Bury.' The first time that the diary mentions the Burys is August 16th, 1825: 'Left Iddesleigh to dine at Dennington – took the hounds with me', but that hardly reads like a first meeting. Russell was friendly with the Southcombes of Rose Ash, one of whose daughters was Penelope's 'best friend' and the Burys owned Colleton, one of the grander houses of Chulmleigh. It would be surprising if Russell had not met Admiral and Mrs Bury and their two daughters at Newton Fellowes' house at Eggesford, or at the Fortescue's at Castle Hill. What is quite clear is that the Burys strongly opposed any match between Penelope and the Curate of South Molton.

Even the edited version of the courtship that the old Russell recounted to Otter Davies suggests this. Davies records that Russell rode from Stock House , the home of an important old Blundellian, Yeatman, to Bath in early 1826. After dining after a day's hunting with Yeatman's pack, Russell rode overnight to Bath, hiring a fresh horse at Warminster in the pitch dark. He rode on to the White Lion Inn at Bath and next morning went round to the Burys' lodgings at No 9 Milsom

Street to arrange to ride out with Penelope and others. When the time for the ride occurred Russell was chagrined to see that, in the light of day, his Warminster hack was a joke of a nag. Eleanor Kerr, a later biographer improves on Otter Davies' story by correctly killing off old Admiral Bury in 1825, but she gives his age as 'over eighty'. He was in fact buried in Bishop's Tawton on April 12th, 1825, aged sixty-eight.

The Admiral died a wealthy man. He had served in many ships, but his only important action had been under Admiral Rodney. It is doubtful whether he won very much prize money. But in his will he left lands in Swimbridge, High Bickington, Chulmleigh, Chawleigh, Winkleigh, Ilfracombe, Lapford, King's Ash, Bishop's Tawton, Ashford and Barnstaple. He was also the senior director of the North Devon Bank, regarded as one of the soundest provincial banks and his will mentions £3600 in cash as well as other moneys. The estate was given partly to his married older daughter Lucy Bencraft, mainly to the enjoyment of his widow Jane Bury, then to be divided between his two daughters.

Russell's diary shows most of the accepted details of his wooing of the heiress Penelope to be either wrong or not to have been the whole truth. He did leave Stock House once for Bath, but he slept at York House, not the White Lion. More importantly the diary shows he made two journeys to Bath in the course of his brief and stormy courtship. The joke horse incident, though, is correct. On Thursday, March 2nd, 1826 Russell wrote ' rode out on Lansdown [Bath] with the Tit and William'. According to the dictionary a 'Tit', amongst other things can mean 'a scruffy horse' or 'a brazen hussy'. In spite of his writing 'with the tit' rather than 'on the tit' one must assume he had the equine rather than the feminine meaning in mind, though things were a little difficult in early March and, to his mind, Penelope may have merited such a description. However Davies was probably wrong in recording that Russell rode the 'tit' in Penelope's company as the diary is quite clear that only his brother William was there.

So to the facts. Penelope had been born in 1799 to Captain and Mrs Richard Incledon. He took the name Bury on inheriting from the last of the Burys of Lapford in 1804, which inheritance brought him Colleton Manor in Chulmleigh, a delightful Jacobean house. Her parents had married in 1792 when her father was thirty-five and her mother thirty-eight and was probably a prudent affair between two families of roughly equal status. Richard Incledon was the third son of Chichester Incledon, a lawyer who had died at Exeter in 1771. The Incledons were an extensive and well connected North and West Devon family. Chichester Incledon's older sister married a Harris of Lifton and

Stowford so that Russell had in-law connections with his hunting companion of the later 1820s, Charles Arthur Harris. Chichester Incledon's mother had been a Chichester of Youlston and a cousin of his, Amy Incledon, had married Charles Chichester of Hall, the father of the Jane Chichester that his son Richard Incledon married in 1792. Penelope's parents were from families that had intermarried for at least three generations. Penelope's older sister, Lucy, was born in 1793 and at forty-four Jane Bury may well have been surprised to find herself once again with child.

When Russell began courting Penelope, Jane Bury was seventy-one and recently widowed. Penelope was twenty-six. In the circumstances Jane Bury probably put up the best fight possible against a match she considered unsuitable between her wealthy daughter and a curate, who, although not penniless, had a name which was a bye word in hunting circles and whose conduct of clerical duty was minimal. On Russell's side was a charm and openness of manner, many friends and the entree to the best local houses. Russell hunted regularly with the current Sir Arthur Chichester of Youlston and was chummy with many of the young bloods of the county.

It is difficult to say conclusively when Russell and Penelope first met. The Admiral was a subscriber to the Staghounds and may have been a hunting man. Russell had often hunted the Chulmleigh area and was increasingly a companion of Newton Fellowes of Eggesford. His diary tells of a Chulmleigh Club Week starting on October 7th, 1823, another on October 12th, 1824 and again on February 21st 1825, on the second day of which the chase ended at Colleton. He may also have met Penelope as early as June 11th, 1824, when he attended a big ball at Castle Hill, the Fortescue mansion only three miles from Admiral Bury's other and more regularly used home at Dennington in Swimbridge. Another possibility could have been July 25th, 1825 when he 'dined at Hannaford with the Southcombes. Swimbridge Revel.'

However the doubt ends on August 16th, 1825. 'Left Iddesleigh [where his brother William was acting as his father's curate] to dine at Dennington – took the hounds with me.' As far as the evidence of the diary goes this was his first visit to Dennington, though one must assume that he was on familiar terms with the Burys, as, even for Russell, turning up to visit an all female household with a pack of hounds would have been a little odd. One must also assume that he and Penelope were already reasonably thick for on the next day he dined at Hall, and on Friday 19th he dined at Dennington again. Unusually in the next week he only hunted once and in the following week only twice, though he did go to a wrestling match. Perhaps he was already in love.

On September 3rd the plot thickens. 'Domi. Went to Dennington with Scott and dined there'. The latter sentence was written in pencil and was probably a later addition, being one of only two entries in pencil. Scott was also mentioned in the entries of August 31st and September 2nd. He may have been one of the Scotts of Cockenham, a house to the north of South Molton where Russell dined on August 5th. One of the late Admiral Bury's partners in the North Devon Bank was 'Scott', probably a connection by marriage as one of the Admiral's older sisters had married a Charles Scott of Cornwall. This Scott may have been her son and therefore Penelope's first cousin. Two months later , on October 10th, Russell wrote 'killed a brace of hares on Great Heale, dined with Henry Bawden to AVOID Scott and went to Knowstone.' The next day he hunted with Jack Froude and 'came home to dine with G. Pearse, met Scott on my way going to Crediton'. Was this the rising passing the falling suitor.

There is some evidence that between August 16th and October 10th Russell won Penelope's heart, probably cutting out poor Scott. After a fortnight hunting at Cruwys Morchard and Torrington Russell had returned to South Molton on September 24th: 'Domi in the morn – sent hounds to Cheriton, went to Dennington and returned with Misses Bury and Southcombe to South Molton.' This was a Saturday, so Sunday the 25th found Russell and Miss Bury in South Molton. It must be supposed that she attended his church and that he preached with her in the congregation, she twenty-six he rising thirty those many years ago. What was his text? Had they already declared themselves or was the tenderness yet unspoken? Did they both pray for the same thing?

Whatever the answers Russell followed his hounds to Cheriton Fitzpaine. Previously such visits had been week long affairs, but this time something, love or the horn colic, brought him back to South Molton mid morning on Tuesday 27th. 'Rode to Whitechapel, Blastridge and North Molton with Misses Southcombe and Bury. Dined at Mrs Southcombe's rode to Kerscot Hill in the eve with Misses S and B to see the latter a little on her journey !!!! Dies mihi carissima!!' Back he went to Cheriton on Wednesday. Kerscott is 9 of the 10 miles from the Southcombes at North Molton to Dennington, so it was not a 'little on her journey at all', and probably a lovely ride on a fine late September's evening.

However 'carissima' the 'dies' may have been, Russell's routine was not broken again until October 4th when he 'went to Dennington and slept there – dies felicissima'. It was on the following 10th October that he felt it prudent to avoid Scott who then was on his way to Dennington. Russell's use of 'felicissima' probably meant 'full of good luck' in the sense of things falling out right and must have meant either that he had been accepted by Penelope or approved as an 'intended' by Mrs Bury, or both.

From now on the road to matrimony, though at times bumpy, dramatic and anxious, was traversed at a gallop, with the hounds in full cry occasionally drowning the cooing of the turtle doves. Russell's diary entries for the weekend after Scott's dismissal are so piquant that they deserve full quotation: 'Friday 14th October. Left home for Woolhanger [three miles south of Lynmouth] at 5 o'clock in the morn, killed two brace of hares, very good scent, dined at the Crown, Lynmouth. Spent the eve with Mrs and Miss Bury and Mrs Hewlett at the Valley!! [presumably the Valley of the Rocks].
Saturday 15th. Perambulated in the morning before breakfast on Mr Sandford's walk cum mea puella [notice that 'mea'], took the hounds to the Valley of the Rocks, returned to the Public and rode to Horner's Neck with – . – – [Penelope?], dined at the Valley with the ladies, delightful day!!
Sunday 16th. Perambulated as yesterday, remained till half past eight and came home on Billy in one hour and ten minutes. Things rather in confusion at home it being Sunday.' Too true! Besides the normal services he had a baptism to do. The registers also state that he buried someone and married a couple on the 15th, which was impossible, so, perhaps in his haste and confusion, he just got the date wrong. A hectic day.

The whole episode may repay closer attention. Lynmouth was then quite a tourist resort and his quarry was essentially human not vulpine. It seems very odd that he took the hounds with him but perhaps they were there to explain his presence at Lynmouth on a 'fancy meeting you here' line, some prearranged plot between himself and Penelope, bored at the prospect of a trip to Lynmouth in the company of Mrs Hewlett and her seventy-one-year-old mother. One must wonder whether pre breakfast perambulations in mid October had Mama's sanction. My own guess is that Mama did not know how far things had progressed between her daughter and the Curate of South Molton and she did not regard that Esau of a curate as a potential son-in -law. There is also the possibility that Russell had intended to set off earlier to return to South Molton church in good time and that it was Penelope who waylaid him and made him so late back.

From then on his courtship was full of ups and downs. On October 21st Russell dined at the Southcombe's with the Burys and Mrs Hewlett, but no more meetings occurred until November 1st when he 'went to Kerscot Hill, met P.B.' Presumably this was a tryst, about which Mrs Bury was ignorant. Then either Mama summoned John Russell Senior or he asked Mrs Bury to receive him at Dennington.

'Friday 4th November. Went to Dennington, met the Governor there, spent a delightful day, rode with Mrs B and the Governor to Chittlehampton etc [where Mrs Bury's trusted brother was Rector] . Hewlett came to dinner. Slept there.

Saturday 5th. Had a coye in the Hermitage before breakfast, came home [a 'coye' is a tryst and the Hermitage was a folly in the grounds of Castle Hill].' Then followed a Chulmleigh Club Week interrupted on Wednesday 9th 'Domi in the morn, went to Stag's Head to meet P, rode with her to Leary and Highdown etc, came home'. This was a melancholy ride as Penelope would have reported that her mother was removing her to Bath, out of Russell's reach, to meet other more acceptable suitors, for on 'Monday 14th P came [to South Molton], things rather unpleasant, in her way to Bath. Went to Tiverton to get an interview with her, but did not succeed.'

So on November 4th 1825 John Russell, Vicar of Crediton, Rector of Iddesleigh and Jacobstowe and Perpetual Curate of St Juliot visited Dennington, surely a significant event in an early nineteenth century courtship. It is clear that the negotiations did not go well. By all accounts Russell senior was an agreeable man, though no one has a good or a bad word for Mrs Bury. Personalities apart there can have been only one reason for the breach – the state of the Russell family finances. It seems improbable that the Whiggery of the late Admiral Bury and the notorious Toryism of Russell *père* could have caused much friction. An interesting survival in the Devon Record Office is a draft will made by the older Russell, dated 1825. Obviously a prudent man of over sixty makes a will, but it is stretching coincidence too far to suppose that this draft is not a trace of the marriage negotiations of November 1825. 'Well, Mr Russell, what can you settle on your son if he marries my daughter.' Mr Russell could only quote the £800 handed over to his son in 1820, probably already spent, and the promise eventually of the estates of his grandfather J. Terrell. Quite inadequate to keep Penelope in the state which Mrs Bury thought proper, so back to Bath and the matrimonial circus for Penelope.

A lesser man might have given up. Diary entries are brief for a week, but the hunting descriptions are normal again towards the end of November. Christmas 1825 was spent in a welter of hunting and dining out. Monday January 30th was spent hunting near High Bickington. The meet on the 31st was at the Rackenford Bell. They found a fox and chased him to 'Spurway Mills, Oakford, West Taps, Allshears, Hockwell Moor and hunted him in the Moor adjoining Old Way. He went to Hockwell Moor, Hockwell House, Anstey Parsonage, Harmerwood, Stream Combe, Dulverton Common where he got into the Road, which he ran, occasionally turning down wind on the heath and at the very best pace to Smallcombe where he sunk the Bottom, and was run into in gallant style in Brimmacombe Court – a burst of fifty five minutes after he was fresh found. Dined at Elton's with Baillie and Col. Robbertson [sic] and Chichester – slept at The Tuns.

Wednesday February 1st. Rode to Taunton, left my mare at the Castle, jump'd on the coach and arrived at the White Hart, Bath, at half past eight, drank tea and went to bed.'

This dash to Bath must have been unpremeditated. After all the Rackenford Bell fox might have headed in any direction. At the end of the day Russell must have been tired, his horse exhausted and his clothes filthy. He can hardly have ridden out from South Molton to Rackenford with an overnight bag just in case he ended up at Dulverton. The clues to what happened may lie around Elton's candle-lit table. Elton had appeared five times in the diary before this. In January 1824 Elton had mounted Russell on 'Woodpecker' for hunting near Tiverton and they had dined together before going on to a Tiverton ball . In June Russell 'rode a match or two on Tiverton Race Course for Worth against Elton' and in July he had 'tried Buller's horse for Elton and wrote ditto'. The entry for March 12th 1825 shows Elton to have been a Chulmleigh Club habitué. So Elton was definitely a friend of Russell's and a man with a previous record of trust in and generosity to Russell. Colonel Robertson of Tiverton sent two sons to Blundell's in the 1820s, but nothing else is known of him. Chichester may well have been Sir Arthur Chichester of Youlston, with whom Russell often hunted and who was a relative and not so distant neighbour of Mrs Bury. Baillie is first mentioned in the diary on September 28th 1824, when they both dined with 'Nimrod' at Exeter. Russell next met Baillie on October 2nd 1825 when he 'went to Cheriton, did the duty and return'd home, call'd at Baillie at Worlington in my way who had shot his finger off'. On January 9th 1826 Baillie had dined with Russell at South Molton. There were two Baillies at Blundell's in Russell's time, Alexander, arriving in 1806 and leaving in 1815, was three years younger than Russell and Evan, 1811-19, five years younger and their father lived in Bristol. So a possible explanation of events may have been: recent intelligence from Bath via Baillie, don't worry about silly old Jane Bury from Sir Arthur, a loan of a fresh horse from Elton and some up and at 'em spirit from the Colonel. Anyway he dashed off to Bath, waking the next day, February 2nd, at the White Hart no doubt excited and anxious.

'Thursday, February 2nd. Went to No 9 Milsom St., [the Bury lodgings] and was received with open arms, spent a most happy morning, after the first half hour, dined at the White Hart. William Arundel came to me in the eve, went to the Rooms, danced one set with P and chatted the rest of the eve away, slept at the White Hart.

Friday 3rd. Spent the morning at No 9, the weather both within and without rather tempestuous in the upper stories, took a dismal leave of P at 3 o'clock'. Russell returned to Taunton the next day. It is obvious that Mrs Bury had thrown a fit at the reappearance of Russell and, once she had recovered her wind, was responsible for the tempest in the upper storeys. The 'dismal leave' must reflect Russell realisation that the affair was blighted by her intransigence. Sunday saw him back at South Molton. Unfortunately he never recorded his thoughts in his diary and there are no clues to explain his next visit to Bath. His first visit must have been unpremeditated, but the second was premeditated. His move began on Sunday February 25th. 'Domi in the morn. Rode to Tiverton and slept at Dayman's.

Monday 26th. Rode from Tiverton to Stock House [Sherborne].

Tuesday 27th. Found a fox with the little Pack, which Templer sold to Mr Yeatman, in Elscombe Wood nr Wincanton, ran him king's pace twenty minutes and kill'd him.

Wednesday. At Pelham with Yeatman's harriers, a beautiful run and took her up alive, left them and rode to Bath. Met William and Baillie at the York House, slept there.' This was the journey he would have made via Warminster, picking up the joke horse.

'Thursday. Called at No 9, spent a few hours there, and rode out on Lansdowne with the Tit and William, dined at the York House. Met Mrs at the rooms in the eve.

Friday. Left Bath at 5 o'clock in the morn.'

One would very much like to know what he and 'Mrs' had talked about. It is clear that relations were still strained even after Penelope had returned to Dennington. When Russell had visited in 1825, he had invariably dined or slept or both. In March 1826 he and Penelope made contact but apparently he did not enter the house. 'March 27th. Went to Dennington, walk'd round Ditto with P till 4 o'clock, went from thence to King's Nympton…

Thursday 30th. Went to Dennington, call'd on Mrs Bencraft [Penelope's older sister Lucy] with P and rode the whole morn, dined and slept at Riccard's.

Saturday, April 1st. Rode with P to E. Buckland, Stone Cross and home'. This is all in marked contrast to the previous Autumn when he always 'dined' or 'slept' at Dennington on every visit.

Three things helped to bring about the marriage within two months Firstly, but unquantifiably, was the pressure brought to bear on Mama by Penelope, who was obviously in love with her curate and who must have been putting pressure on Mrs Bury. Her sister Lucy may have helped too. Secondly, Russell was badly hurt in a fall while hunting from Landue, the house of his friend Tom Phillips. 'Thursday, March 6th. Met at Tetcot with parts of Templer's little and gt pack, broke two ribs by a fall from Monkey and was put to bed at Tetcot'. On the 8th he moved to Landue and spent five days there, recuperating. Remarkably he was hunting again on April 14th. It is possible that this accident acted as a spur to Penelope's affection and determination.

Thirdly and most importantly a Commodore Sharland suddenly appeared on the scene. On April 24th Russell 'went to Dennington, enjoyed a very pleasant walk with P – called at the Commodore's'. The Commodore lived at Wrimstone, less than a mile south of Dennington. On April 28th Russell 'dined at the Commodore's, met P, pleasant eve, slept there.' Presumably the Commodore persuaded Mrs Bury to allow Russell and Penelope to ride to King's Nympton and Colleton the next day 'a most delightful morning.' On May 1st he 'dined and slept at the Commodore's, walked with P'. He hunted with the Commodore in the Lynmouth area from May 3rd to 7th. It seems that the Commodore, who I guess was a trusted friend and neighbour of the late Admiral Bury, had given Russell his seal of approval.

The rapprochement, when it came, was rapid. On Sunday May 7th Russell attended Swimbridge, not South Molton church, presumably in the company of the Commodore and both Mrs and Miss Bury. On the 8th he and Penelope dined with Penelope's sister Lucy at Barnstaple and on the 10th the marriage was arranged: 'Had an interview with Mrs Bury at William Law's [a lawyer, whose offices were in The Square Barnstaple], everything went off better than I expected'. The note of satisfaction, even of triumph is evident on Thursday May 11th 'Rode to Barum with P, the first day of the cricket club, dined at Dennington !!!!!'. Further to substantiate the Commodore's role as Pandar to the betrothed couple, he now accompanied Russell on shuttle diplomacy between Swimbridge and Iddesleigh, either to vet the Rectory as a suitable home for the married couple, or to settle things with John Russell senior. 'Saturday 12th. Went to Iddesleigh with the Commodore', and they visited Iddesleigh again on the 22nd.

After his re-entry into Dennington Russell dined there regularly and the rest of May was a merry month. 'Monday 14th. Returned from Iddesleigh to Wrimstone, walk'd with P in the eve.

Tuesday 15th. Rode with P to South Molton, dined at Dennington with the Commodore.

Wednesday 16th. Dined at Wrimstone with William [his brother who would officiate at the wedding].

Thursday 17th. Rode with P and Bill to Barum, dined at Dennington.

Friday 18th. Dined at Riccard's.

Saturday 19th. Spent the morning at Dennington, dined at Lucy's.

Sunday 21st. Did the duty at Swimbridge, dined at Dennington.

Monday 22nd. Tried the Taw with Nott, Eastmond and the Commodore after which the latter and I rode to Iddesleigh. No sport.

Tuesday 23rd. Returned from Iddesleigh, met P at Wrimstone, dined at Hole's South Molton.

Wednesday 24th. Returned from South Molton, spent the day at Wrimstone etc etc.

Thursday 25th. With P riding and walking.

Friday 26th. Ditto ditto ditto.

Saturday 27th. Went to Iddesleigh, returned home early and spent the remainder of the day with P.

Sunday 28th. Did the duty at Landkey and Swimbridge, dined at Dennington.

Monday 29th. Spent the day at Dennington and Wrimstone, met William Law in the eve and signed the Marriage Settlements.

Tuesday 30th May 1826. Took Penelope Incledon Bury to Wife, adjourned with ditto in a chariot and four greys, furnished by Pratt of 'Old London' Exeter, to South Molton and Tiverton and slept at the George Inn, Bridgwater!!!' Then in a smaller hand he inserted 'Boy born 31st May, christened John Bury.' The marriage service was performed by his younger brother William, who was either writing with a poor pen or was ill, as his writing looks like that of an old man. The witnesses were Lionel Bencraft, the husband of Penelope's older sister Lucy, and perhaps Henry Sharland, the Commodore, but the signature is illegible.

Chapter Six

THE IDDESLEIGH YEARS

John and Penelope Russell's marriage lasted almost forty-nine years before Penelope died in January 1875. In the first three years two sons were born, John Bury and Richard Bury. John arrived exactly a year after the wedding and is said to have been buried in May 1828 in Iddesleigh churchyard, and in the early summer of 1998 the author found his stone lying against the north wall of Iddesleigh Church. Richard Bury, always known by his second name, was born on August 23rd, 1828 and, although Penelope was then only twenty-nine, Bury was her last child. There is probably no means of knowing if this infertility caused the Russells any sadness nor do more than speculate at its causes. The first two children were born almost as quickly as biology allows, and then there were no more.

One aspect of the problem is that so little is known of Penelope. There are some slender grounds for supposing that Admiral Bury did not expect her to marry. His will, written about 1824, leaves his property to his wife Jane, but divides his estates into two roughly equal parts for eventual inheritance by his daughters. In the case of Lucy, already married to Stephen Bencraft, the old Admiral was very precise in his provision for her and her children, but there was no sum earmarked as a dowry for Penelope, nor any reservation for any children she might one day have. Although only twenty-five when the will was drawn up, Penelope perhaps was going to look after Mama. Jane Bury had been forty-five when Penelope had been born. Another aspect of the problem is that, having been so regularly mentioned in the diary before their marriage in May 1826, she drops out of it almost entirely after marriage. Between September 1827, when Russell restarted his diary and April 1828, when for some reason he suspended making entries, Penelope was only mentioned five times. When Russell again started making entries in August 1831 she is also hardly mentioned.

It is even difficult to tell whether Penelope is with her mother at Dennington or with her husband at Iddesleigh. After the entry for his wedding day, May 30th 1826 he ruled a line across the page and under it he wrote, 'If I have not been at home since June 17th 1826 (the day I returned from my Wedding Tour and came to Iddesleigh) I ought to have been, and therefore I make no entry till September 1st 1827.' Yet in September 1827 when he entered 'Domi' he meant 'Iddesleigh'. From Iddesleigh on September 19th, 1827 he took 'Penny and Boy' to Rumsom where the Bencraft's lived. And then follows the only passage where she is regularly mentioned:

'Thursday 20th at Rumsom.

Friday 21st at Rumsom, dined with Dr Bignell.

Saturday 22nd. Met the Cry at Umberleigh Bridge, killed four hares. Took the hounds to Great Heale [South Molton], dined at Rumsom.

Sunday Septr 23rd. Preach'd a Charity Sermon at Barum, dined with Mr Glass.

Monday 24th. Hunting on G. Heale, killed three hares.

Tuesday 25th Met Sir Arthur Chichester at Bray, found in Molland Wood, killed under Bradley, a good run.

Wednesday 26th. Hunting at Romansleigh kill'd two hares.

Thursday 27th. Went to Rumsom from South Molton and brought Mrs and Boy to Dennington, dined and slept there. [So presumably he had left Penny with her sister since Sunday.]

Friday 28th. Hunting on G Heale, found only one hare and killed her.

Saturday 29th. Went to Dennington and slept there.

Sunday Septr 30th. Returned home in the morn from Dennington, found William there.

Monday Octbr 1st. Met the Cry on Beacon Hill, Chulmleigh, killed three hares, dined at South Molton, slept at Dennington.

Tuesday 2nd. Brought Mrs and the Boy to South Molton.

Wednesday 3rd. Hunting at Romansleigh. Killed three hares.

Thursday 4th. At South Molton.

Friday 5th. Hunting at Romansleigh, kill'd four hares.

Saturday 6th. Return'd home bag and baggage.'

Penelope returned to Dennington on December 27th and probably stayed there until the end of January 1828. He mentioned her in February when they went to the theatre in Exeter to hear Miss Foote in *Miss Dorillon*. On April 1st he rode with Miss Fisher and Penny to Buckland Filleigh. The diary entries stop on April 12th and only restart in August 1831, continuing until May 1832. In that period Penelope went to Dennington in September and probably returned to Iddesleigh just before Christmas after they had both been to Exeter to hear Paganini play on December 20th. Soon after Christmas they both dined with Lord Clinton at Heanton, then she returned to Dennington and stayed there until March 20th. He escorted her back to Dennington on April 4th.

Whether or not they were almost living apart it is clear that she never came between her husband and his hunting. Taken to a concert and the theatre, fetched and carried to and from Dennington, she is a dim figure, and it would not give a false impression to quote the week starting on September 19th, 1831 'Hunted round the house [Iddesleigh Rectory], kill'd a brace of hares. Rode Cottager. dined with Mr Acland, Barnstaple afterwards.

Tuesday. At Dennington. Penny ill.

Wednesday. Left Dennington at seven, dined at Bodmin at three (chez Pomeroy Gilbert at the Priory).

Thursday. With Phillips at Dunmeer.

Friday. Breakfasted at the Priory. Dined at Iddesleigh, took the pack to Tordown [about to be his new home at Swimbridge] in the eve.

Saturday. Killed a brace of hares at Challacombe, gave them to the farmers, dined at Upcott.'

It would be dangerous to go further than to suggest that Russell took his wife for granted. Nevertheless it is tempting to add two and two and make five when reading Bishop Phllpotts' diary for August 19th, 1831. Russell as friend was accompanying the Rev. Mr Landon of Bishop's Tawton (a first cousin of Penelope's), who was to be seriously reprimanded and admonished for neglect of residence. 'Afterwards I stated the more serious charge of incontinence at Exeter. Landon admitted the affair lasting one year, but said intercourse had ended several months ago, though he gave the woman money in May last. Whether I would proceed against him would depend on what should appear to be the evidence. I made a very serious admonition, which seemed to affect Mr Russell more than the culprit who did not exhibit any indication of penitence, but merely of sorrow and fear'. One is reminded of Templer and the 'horn colic'. Landon had married Jane Chichester, a daughter of Jane Bury's older brother Charles, in 1828 and remained a regular hunting companion of Russell's.

Although the romance of marriage may have soon faded, Russell needed Bury money to provide the resources necessary for hunting. His income of £100 from the curacies of Iddesleigh and Monkokehampton may have been supplemented with a little Russell money, but such help cannot have been very great as a letter from Russell senior to Archdeacon Barnes of Exeter sums up his financial condition.

Crediton, 17th March 1837,

Dear Sir,

It is impossible that I shou'd have forgotten the great liberty I have taken – and equally so that I shou'd ever forget the great obligation your kind indulgence has laid me under!!

I was duly prepared to discharge your bill, when I was beset by those with whom I deal, on seeing that I was about to remove from Crediton, preferring their claims.

Lady-Day is at hand, when I shall be entitled to receive many valuable sums and I give you my honour that I shall wait upon you with the first fruits of them: when I shall have the opportunity of thanking you in person for your unmerited kindness to – my dear Sir, your grateful humble servant,

John Russell.

In June 1866 *Bailey's Magazine* itemised the expenses of an MFH who hunted three days a week as about £1200. It is clear that Russell hunted 'on the cheap'. He never had more than six horses, rather than the 12 Bailey's recommended and he only had an amateur whip, a boy called Sam, whom he had trained himself. Apparently, after the day's hunting was over, he would call Sam into his study, pour out a glass of wine and go over the day's events on a question and answer basis. If Sam showed attentiveness and understanding he got the wine. If not Russell beat him. Some expenses were shared with Charles Harris of Hayne, but it is difficult to see how Russell could have hunted for less than £400 a year in 1866 values, probably little different from those of 1830.

It would be helpful to know exactly what resources he did receive from those marriage settlements drawn up by William Law. By Admiral Bury's will Penelope was to inherit his estates in Swimbridge, High Bickington, Burrington, Chulmleigh and Chawleigh, which in the Land Tax records of 1826 were assessed to pay £42-12-0, giving a declared gross rental of about £225. But she would only receive this property after the death of her mother, who, ironically, only died in 1848 at the great age of ninety-four. However two farms in High Bickington, Ash and Seckington, are recorded in the Land Tax Assessment as being in Penelope's ownership. On December 10th 1827, Russell wrote 'drove Susan Southcombe to Chulmleigh and transacted business with Gould, signed the deeds for the sale of Ash etc etc'. I think it fair to conclude that within eighteen months of marriage Russell had hunted his way through whatever cash he had received as part of Penelope's dowry and was consuming those of her assets which were accessible.

Some of the land in Mrs Bury's ownership was disposed of at this time as well. She sold Golland in Burrington in 1828 and Moortown in Chawleigh in 1832, both farms being part of the estates willed by the Admiral towards Penny. On March 3rd 1828 Russell wrote 'rode to Dennington to see Mrs Bury', the only time he mentioned his mother-in-law in the diary after the wedding. Perhaps the visit was to explain the depths of his financial embarrassment, which had not been bridged by the sale of Ash and Seckington. It may also be that her realisation of Russell's profligacy led to her taking the first steps towards having him appointed to the Perpetual Curacy of Swimbridge and Landkey, a living in the gift of Dean Landon, the father of the adulterer. Her hand was surely behind the last entry of the diary, 'Tuesday May 1st, 1832 Beal took five couple of my hounds to Haccombe [the home of Sir Walter Palk Carew] Tom Hext took 11 couple to Bodmin – both lots to be returned to me whenever I demand them,' which was written a few weeks after he had been translates from Iddesleigh to Swimbridge.

Meanwhile he spent and enjoyed his hunting. Unfortunately his diary entries are briefer than before and his diary has two large gaps, from June 1826 to September 1827 and from May 13th 1828 until August 23rd 1831. The latter gap may be explained by the death of his infant son, John Bury, but the more likely explanation lies in the context of his hunting. In the seasons of 1828-9, 1829-30 and 1830-31 he was hunting on a grand scale with the wealthy and great from Bodmin to Chulmleigh. When his domain shrank again to Iddesleigh and its neighbourhood he reverted to his old book. Somewhere in the accumulations of Pencarrow, Bodmin Priory, Landue, Haccombe, Hayne or Eggesford may lie the hunting diaries of those years – more likely they have perished.

The earlier gap remains a mystery. After the entry that described his wedding day he wrote in a very small hand 'Boy born 31st May 1827!! xned John Bury.' Then there is a line drawn right across the page and he wrote 'If I have not been at home since June 17th, 1826, the day that I returned from my wedding tour and came to Iddesleigh, I ought to have been, and therefore I make no entry till September 1st, 1827.' Probably those words were written on September 1st 1827 and that by then Iddesleigh was 'home', which explains 'ought'. He 'ought' to have been at Iddesleigh and not have been a non-resident. Yet he married, buried and baptised folk in Iddesleigh church after August 1826 and in the neighbouring parish of Monkokehampton after early 1827. Nevertheless we cannot be sure where he was living and even stranger there is no record of John Bury's christening or funeral in the parish records of Swimbridge, Iddesleigh or Bishop's Tawton, though his grave stone has been discovered at Iddesleigh.

However it is quite clear that he was living in Iddesleigh parsonage after September 1827, a house that no longer exists. In the late 1840s, after his father's death the house burnt down and was rebuilt by Pitman, his father's successor as rector. Even Pitman's house no longer exists and all that remains on the site are some substantial outbuildings, which have become a house called 'Devon Lodge', in whose gardens are the traces of larger buildings. The site is superb, approached up a long winding drive of a quarter of a mile with long views beyond Iddesleigh church a mile to the north, spreading in a semicircle to the wide valley of the Okement, running south to Monkokehampton. Most people would regard Iddesleigh as a hamlet – a post office, a pub, a cluster of cob and thatch cottages and what was once a village school. Then as now more people probably lived in the isolated and ancient farmhouses than around the parish church. I doubt if a more rural spot could be found in all England. Although Okehampton and Crediton might resent it, there is no town worthy of the name nearer than Exeter, Barnstaple or Plymouth, the nearest of them being 20 miles away and, in the early nineteenth century, they were very far away indeed. On a clear day from the parish church Dartmoor fills the southern horizon with its strong, round outlines, but in the other directions the farming patch- work of greens, browns and yellows stretches away, unbroken by pylons or urban haze. One is in the heartland of rural Devon and its roots are Saxon deep – about 700 A.D. Eadwig gave the parish its name.

Although far from Penelope's normal haunts, Iddesleigh was home ground for Russell. His grandfather, Michael, had been Rector of Meeth, just across the River Torridge from Iddesleigh, from 1745-90 and doubt- less many of his grandfather's parishioners welcomed the young curate for his sake. His father had been rector of Iddesleigh since 1823 and his brother William had been curate since then. Russell spent the first six days of September 1827 hunting around the Rectory and throughout the 1827-8 season he did most of his hunting close to Iddesleigh, hares being the main quarry.

Foxes are not often mentioned. In the whole season only ten were killed and none of those near Iddesleigh, the nearest being at Passaford south of Hatherleigh. So the stories told by Otter Davies about the vulpicidal tendencies of his new parishioners were probably true. Apparently whenever a fox was discovered the procedure was to ring the church bells or make some other clamour. The human and canine inhabitants of the village would then rush off, dig up and batter to death the enemy. Davies quoted a letter from Russell, presumably in reply to a request for details of his life in Iddesleigh. 'During the winter of my first year at Iddesleigh, the snow at the time lying deep on the ground, a native, Bat Anstey came to me and said, "Hatherley bell is a-ringing,sir!"

"Ringing for what?" I enquired, with a strong misgiving.

"Well, sir, they've a-traced a fox in somewhere, and they've a got the bell a-going to collect the people to shoot 'un.".

"Come, Bat, and tell me where 'tis." I replied.

"In Middlecot earths, sir; just over the Okement."

I was soon on the spot with ten couple of my little hounds, and found, standing around the earths, about a hundred fellows – the scum of the country – headed, I am almost ashamed to say, by two gentlemen, Mr Veale of Passaford and Mr Morris of Fishleigh, the father of Colonel W. Morris of the Light Brigade – that brilliant swordsman in whose memory a monument is erected on Hatherleigh Moor.

I remonstrated with these gentlemen and told them plainly that if they would leave the earths, and preserve foxes for me, I would show them more sport with my little pack in one day than they would see in a whole year by destroying the gallant animal in so un-English a way.

Impressed, apparently, by what I had said, both gentlemen instantly bade me a "good morning" and left; while a few shillings distributed among the crowd induced them to disperse. Then waiting half an hour or so I turned my head towards home, but, before I arrived there, I met a man, open-mouthed, bawling out, "They've a-traced a fox into Brimblecombe; for I hear Dowland bell a-going." So off I set to Dowland in post haste; found out where the fox was lying, turned him out of a furze bush, ran him an hour and forty minutes and picked him up alive before the hounds on the very earths I had just quitted, where a couple of scoundrels had remained on watch and headed him.

The very next day after the run from Brimblecombe a man came from Iddesleigh to inform me that the bell was going at Beaford, and that a fox had been traced into a brake near the hamlet. I let out the hounds at once and hurried to the spot with all speed. On arriving at the brake I found only one man there, who, as a sentinel, was guarding it from disturbance with a watchful eye. I asked him to tell me where the fox was; but he gave me a very impertinent answer, saying "he knawed better than that and wasn't a-going to do no such thing." I kept my temper and, pulling out half-a-crown, I said, "There, my man, I'd have given you that if you'd told me where he was." The fellow's eye positively sparkled at the sight of the silver. "Let me have it then," he replied, "and I will show you where he is to a yard."

I ran him an hour and lost him almost where he was found. Then, just as I was calling the hounds to go home, down came a crowd of men, women and children, the former mostly from the inn, to see this fox murdered. Many of them had brought their loaded guns, were full of beer and eager for the fray. And when they discovered that I had disturbed THEIR fox, their language was anything but choice. A strapping young fellow, one of the principal farmers of the parish came up to me, and said "Who are you, sir, to come here and spoil our sport? You have no business here!"

"As much as you have", I replied; "for the owner has given me leave to hunt over this estate, and I mean doing so, too, whenever I please. So get a horse, come out with me, and I'll show you some fine sport, if only you'll give up shooting foxes."

"We'll shoot them whenever we can; that I'll promise you," he said in an angry tone. At that moment one of the hounds began to howl. I looked round, saw she was in pain, and asked, in a threatening manner, "Who kicked that hound?" No-one spoke for half a minute, when a little boy said, pointing to another, "That boy kicked her."

"Did he?" I exclaimed; "then 'tis lucky for him he is a LITTLE boy."

"Why?" asked the farmer with whom I had previously been talking. "Because", I replied, "if a MAN had kicked her I would have HORSE-WHIPPED him on the spot!"

"You would find that a difficult job, if you tried it," was his curt answer. I jumped off my horse, threw down my whip, and said, "Who's the man to prevent me?" Not a word was spoken. I stood my ground, and one by one the crowd retired, the young farmer amongst the number; and from that day forward I secured for myself and successors not only the co-operation and goodwill, but also the friendship, of some of the best fox-preservers that the county of Devon, or any other county, has seen.'

Such tactics could not but win the adherence of the brutish peasantry and the support of the local farmers and squires. Before long Russell was hunting up and down the Torridge and Okement, but foxes only slowly became more numerous. Tradition has it that these Iddesleigh years were the most glorious of Russell's long career, when he hunted from Chulmleigh to Bodmin, with kennels at Iddesleigh, Hayne House and Tetcott. Clerical pugilism may have won over the locals, but something more would have been needed to gain the friendship and support of the owners of the great estates. Initially his hunting territory was confined by Newton Fellowes at Eggesford and the Reverend Peter Glubb near Torrington. Newton Fellowes gave him some coverts and old friendships, perhaps developed in Chulmleigh Club Weeks, soon widened his horizons. Of particular importance were Tom Phillips of Landue near Launceston, John Morth Woolcombe of Ashbury near Okehampton and Charles Arthur Harris of Hayne at Stowford .

Russell had known Tom Phillips of Landue, formerly of the 7th Hussars, definitely since the early 1820s and probably the families had known each other since the Calstock times. Russell's diary regularly mentions visits to Landue and in October 1827 Phillips spent a long weekend at Iddesleigh. Until recently, of the houses to which Russell was a frequent visitor only Landue remained in its original state. It lies about four miles from Launceston on the Callington road and is the result of a rebuilding between 1690 and 1710. The house fits snug into a south facing site looking down the valley of the Lowley brook, the A388 kept out of sight by some discrete folds in the ground. The south facade, with its two storeys of nine large windows is very imposing, but it is basically a family house of 'five bedrooms and two reception'. On the northern side there is a dramatic and older hall, part of the original house. The kitchen area, the ten attic bedrooms for servants and the enormous nursery wing show that we are not in Selsdon. A recent owner who died in the early 1990s as a young boy met one of Tom Phillips' daughters and the rooms are probably very much as Russell knew them – simple, generously proportioned in an unfussy late eighteenth century Classical style.

Although Phillips had wide Cornish connections, the person generally held to have played the key role in enlarging Russell's Iddesleigh realm was Charles Arthur Harris. A previous Harris of Hayne had been Master of the Household to George II and George III and a connection of Robert Walpole's who had made a large fortune from public office. This Master of the Houshold died son-less in 1767 and the entailed estate, less Hayne, went to a cousin William Arundell, one of whose descendants was William Arundell Harris Arundell of Lifton Park on the Cornish border. Born in 1794 he lost his father at the age of four and his mother before he was of age and he became a spectacular ne'er do well. Local tradition claimed that he would bet on anything, even on snail races. Such gambling led to bankruptcy and an impecunious retreat to Ostend. He had some as yet unrevealed connection with Russell's brother-in-law, the lawyer and banker Bencraft for, on March 16th 1832, Russell went from Iddesleigh 'to Lifton Park and back for Bencraft'.

Russell met Charles Harris of Hayne definitely at a Chulmleigh Club Week in 1826 when Harris was twenty-five and Russell thirty-one, though they had probably met earlier. Both had recently married. Harris was one of the children of the Romantic Movement and he lapsed easily into hero worship. He rebuilt Hayne with the most delicate spires, crenellations and turrets and double-barrelled his name with a baronial 'Mohun'. Turn off the A 30 at Stowford at the Harris Arms, go over the hill and there lies Hayne. Here the returning huntsmen, hacking through the twilight park, would have entered the hall, mounted the grand staircase to the pillared landing and on up to the bedrooms before returning, refreshed, to the state rooms on the first floor, huge with pendant plaster ceilings and gothick ribbings. Below the servants would be preparing to serve dinner in the olde baronial dining hall.

Even the surrounds are 'gothick'. In the park, near the west gate, is a drunken pillar, memorial to Nick Down, huntsman who, one night, hearing an uproar in the kennels, went to sort out the fuss and was eaten alive by the hounds. About 1865 a page boy in Hayne was murdered while a large house-party was in residence. Inevitably a guest dreamed that his body had been buried by a great oak in the park, the site was dug and the butler confessed. Ghosts, whether of the page, the dreaming guest or the butler, haunt the spot. Hayne was and is that sort of a place.

But the most evocative of what Hayne has to offer is St Hubert's Hall. A broad path leads through rhododendrons next the standing stones of a gateway, one with the hangers still in place, then a gentle serpentine path will rise to a dramatic stone arch of two self-supporting granite slabs. This is the entrance to an old quarry that Charles Harris developed into 'St Hubert's Hall'. Around its sides he levelled paths to give access to twenty-two stalls, each one dedicated to one of his companions. Over each stall was hung a fox's mask, a shield with the appropriate arms and a motto. George Templer's motto was 'Templa quam delecta'. Tom Phillips had 'Palmam qui meruit ferat', John Morth Woolcombe of Ashbury 'Stat promissa fides'. Harris himself had 'Ready aye ready' and Russell's was in Greek, a description by Aeschylus of Agamemnon 'Leader of Men'.

Harris' hero-worship of Russell led to his suggesting the uniting of their packs, but leaving Russell in full charge. Davies records the arrangements thus, 'They struck hands at once; the offer being accepted by Russell subject to the following reservation, namely, that the hounds should belong to him, and that he alone should hunt and control them, terms to which the younger and less experienced sportsman very sensibly agreed. Accordingly on a given day in 1827 the two packs met at Five Oaks, near Okehampton, in all about seventy couple, which Russell, knowing to a handful of meal the value of every hound, quickly drafted down to 35 couple. With this lot he proposed hunting the country alone, giving the country two days a week, with an occasional bye-day according to circumstances.'

Russell's diary can confirm much of this. On November 3rd, 1827

'Hunting on Park and Fursdon etc. Killed three hares. A. Harris came in the morn. Had the drafts'. A further, if vague, exchange took place on March 24th 1828 , 'Met A Harris at 5 Oaks with his pack, selected ... couple and brought them home'. Some of these may well have comprised the remnants of George Templer's pack. However Harris is mentioned surprisingly rarely in Russell's diary. Perhaps the creator of St Hubert's Hall was fun in small doses; 'gothick' can be tiresome.

Although Russell had hunted in the Bodmin area in his bachelor days, Harris enthusiasm, Phillips' friendship and the connection with the Reverend Pomeroy Gilbert of Bodmin Priory might have been influential in opening up the wide covers of Tetcott and Pencarrow to Russell's hounds. It is also possible that his father's appointment and indeed his own, to the Curacy of St Juliot records a connection with the Molesworths of Pencarrow. In these years Russell enjoyed his Cornish visits, which, if Harris and Davies are to be believed, passed into local folklore. Harris, in his book *Letters on the Past and Present Foxhunters of Devonshire* wrote 'When the Tetcott and Hayne districts were hunted for a fortnight together, the whole population of the country turned out to meet Mr Russell at the home fixtures. No farmer within the adjoining or distant parishes, who had a horse or pony, failed to be present; labour was comparatively suspended, and even the women put on their Sunday bonnets and shawls to go and see Mr Russell find a fox. The houses in the neighbourhood were full of guests, and these hunting meetings rather possessed the character of triumphal ovations than the character of ordinary fixtures. Petitions were made by the farmers to arrange the meets so as not to interfere with the Tavistock market, and a sale of stock was not exactly put off, but the advertisement of it was delayed and changed until after the Russell fortnight. And why was all of this? Common sense must point out that a dwarf pack of foxhound, however good they might be, was not the true reason for such a display of hunting popularity. It was the man and the man alone, that caused this general feeling, and gave surety that with a fox on foot Russell was certain to account for him. In the first season the country was rather thinly supplied with foxes; yet, out of 32 found above ground, 28 were killed, two were earthed and two were lost.

'That which most pleased the generality of the hunting men, and especially the moor farmers, was the acute intelligence which this egregious sportsman displayed in everything relating to the habits of a fox, his mode of finding and of getting to him in strong coverts. One of the secrets of his great success was the fact that, with an ordinary scent, his hounds had almost beaten their fox before he got away; and his cheery mode of hunting them in covert was most exhilarating. The celerity with which he effected an object which had been determined upon in his mind was as the whirlwind; no hesitation marred the precipitance of action, and the hounds, confiding in their huntsman, flew to him at the slightest sign of command. At one of the meetings at Hayne, Newton Plantation and gorse – a strictly preserved covert – had been drawn blank, and the hounds, after crossing the river under Milford, were going on through the meadows to draw Arraycot Wood, when the keen eye of Russell detected, in passing by an overgrown hedgerow, the branch of a briar that had been displaced and caught on the branch of a thorn by the passage of an animal. He touched the branch slightly with his whip, it gave way and returned to its original position. Calling his little terrier "Vic", he took her up on his saddle, cheered her on to the hedgerow, and in a few minutes out came a fox that gave a capital run to Townly, Eastlake, Wonnacott, Southwick Moor, Northcombe and Wetherdon, earthing in Henford Wood.

'Again, on another occasion, a large party had gone from Heanton to a bye near Potheridge. A deep covert on the banks of the Torridge, reputed and known to be a sure find, had failed to furnish a fox. It was unmistakable, for even "Daphne" came out without showing a symptom of scent, and Russell rode down to the lower end of a grass field, outside the wood, to call his hounds away. There happened to be a large thistle close to the side of old "Cottager", and as Russell remained quiescent for a moment, horn in hand, something peculiar in the thistle attracted his attention. Calling to a countryman, he said, "Will you have a shilling, my dear chap?" "Oh, e'es – sure," grinned the clod. "Then come here quickly, kneel down, and smell the water in the upper cup of the thistle – d'ye see? Sweet – eh?" "Oh! ah! – e'es sure – oh verra!", chuckling inwardly at having the best of a pleasant bargain. "Now down lower, in the middle one." In went the nose down, down, snuffling up the water. "All right, eh?" "Oo, oo, oih, ah, Chroist Jasis!" "We have him Arthur [Harris]!", exclaimed Russell, and in he went again with his hounds and found him curled up in his kennel; and one of the fastest runs of the season ensued for an hour and forty minutes, with a kill.

'The relation of this anecdote to a large party at Cobham Park, the residence of the late Mr Harvey Combe, then master of the Old Berkeley Hounds, brought a cheer of delight from Osbaldeston. It was this speciality of the man, the mastery in detail of every particularity regarding hounds and foxes, that led to a series of continuous successes which have made the name of Russell conspicuous in England as the pre-eminent sportsman of the West. There was an identification between himself and his hounds, a brisk confidence on their part and a thorough knowledge on his of the peculiarity and temper of each, that gave a combination of power in the field of which it would be well if the example were more frequent. When the celebrated scream was heard, and those who have heard it can bear witness to its thrilling effect, whatever may have been the scent on which the hounds were running, they left it to fly to the well accustomed and well understood voice, which never failed to cheer them on the true line. No flashy holiday hunter, no mute hound ever had a second feed of meal willingly in his kennel. But never let it be supposed that with a flying fox on foot Mr Russell was disposed to hunt rather than to chase him. No one made more daring casts, or was more eager to get near to his fox by a forward movement; and in this he was assisted by a perfect acquaintance with the nature and ways of the wild animal he pursued. Herein consisted that principal cause of superiority even over huntsmen of repute, and in this part of the science, which he had learnt from his able tutor, George Templer, he was and is [1861] unrivalled. To these more immediate attributes of excellence may be added an indomitable perseverance, with a patience in difficulty which usually had its reward; and when, from adverse causes, an absence of sport was unavoidable, a constant fund of good humour and an amiable hilarity dispelled that solemn sadness that often looms over a disappointed field.

'When Michael Angelo was called upon to build the temple of St Peter in Rome, on ascending the hill above Florence, at his departure, he turned towards the Duomo, the splendid work of Brunelleschi, and exclaimed, " Come te se poso, meglio di te mai." So likewise may it be said of Mr Russell – that, possibly, there may be found sportsmen equally good and true – but a better or more consummate one there cannot or was never known to be.'

His diary includes a Cornish visit from March 3rd to March 15th, 1828. 'Monday March 3rd. Took the hounds to Tetcot, dined and slept at Landue.

Tuesday. Found a fox in Beer Down, earth'd him in Panson in half an hour. Best pace – bolt'd him and killed him at Dinnecary. One hour and forty minutes – a beautiful run and very fast.

Wednesday 7th. Hunted with Philips near the house. Killed a brace of hares.

Thursday. Found again in Beer Down and killed in one hour and fifty minutes in cover. He broke twice but was headed each time.

Friday. Came home.

Saturday. Met the hounds from home at Hatherleigh, drew blank and returned home.

Sunday. Domi.

Monday. Went to Bodmin.

Tuesday. Found in Divick [Deviock?] and earthed in one hour and five minutes. Gained her in ten minutes. Gave her to the hounds.

Wednesday. A beautiful day with P. Gilbert on the Moor.

Thursday. Found in Dunmere and killed close to the Racecourse in fifty minutes. A perfect blaze. Found a second in Park Wood, went to ground immediately, gained her and turned her down close to Washaway and earthed her in Hillugan, a burning scent.

Friday. Killed a hare near the Jamaica Inn with P.G. and dined and slept at Landue.

Saturday. Hunted with Phillips at Ivy House. Three good runs and came home.'

However these diary fragments cannot confirm either Davies' Mine-shaft Story or the account of the Deviock Wood Trio. The Mine-shaft story runs thus. 'In the spring of 1831, the young baronet, Sir William Molesworth, then in his twenty-first year, having invited a large party of gentlemen to meet Phillips and the Landue hounds at Pencarrow for a fortnight's hunting, the house was filled to the rafters. The few survivors of that meeting will never forget the 16th of February, when a fox was found at Polbrock, near the riverside, every hound breaking away almost on his back, bringing him over the paling into Pencarrow Park, and by the Roman mounds away to Helland Wood; thence tearing on with a burning scent over the virgin soil of the vast rough enclosure, they carried a grand head and, dashing over the boundary wall, broke out on the moor and on to the Launceston to Bodmin road, where they dropped into slow hunting and then threw up.

'The road was of granite; but a hound called "Memory", with nose well down, held on, faintly feathering; the rest were hopelessly at fault. Phillips, impatient, was turning to cast them towards the Tors north-wards, when Russell exclaimed "Do, pray, give her time." At length a patch of wet ground gave her chance, she dropped her stern, and at the same time throwing her tongue, she dashed over the heather bank on to Temple Moor and away over that grand waste of heather. At the boundary fence above Trebatha the hounds caught a view and instantly as if by a stroke of magic they and the fox vanished from the scene. It seemed to the foremost riders that the earth had opened her jaws and swallowed them alive; and such was the case; the shaft of an old mine lay open, and they had fallen into utter darkness, deep engulfed. The fox, indeed, had clambered onto a broken beam, but three of the leading hounds were swimming about in the dark water at the bottom of the mine, some seven fathoms deep; while the rest of the pack had stopped short of the abyss and scrambled out.

'In a few minutes some miners appeared, but not a man of them would go down, fearing the dangers of the decayed framework of that precipitous shaft. Not so, however Jack Russell, who, with a knotted rope in one hand and his riding whip in the other, lowered himself, amid a shower of loose earth and stones, to the beam on which the fox was crouching. Then running the thong through the keeper of his whip, and fixing the noose round the animal's neck, he shouted aloud, "Haul away. I've got him!", and in half a minute he and the fox were landed again on terra firma.

"Save him, Phillips; he is a gallant fellow and deserves his life" begged Russell. But Phillips sternly tossed him to the hounds.

Then to save the three brave brutes now struggling in the pit from a longer immersion, Russell was again prepared to go to the rescue, had not Colonel Gilbert persuaded a miner with a capful of silver, to go down.'

Davies also told the story of the Deviock Trio which occurreed on another 16th February, but in 1879, when Russell found three foxes together in Deviock Wood, near Bodmin, and killed all three before the sun set on Brownwilly Tors. 'A brace broke cover at once, going away like a loving pair, side by side; while a third stole off without being viewed, and put his head straight for the moor. Breaking on their very brushes, the pack stuck to the former, pelting after them like a storm of hail; when, after a short burst, the foxes separated, and so did the hounds; Russell sticking to one division and screaming to his field to stop the other. Stop them indeed! The best horse that ever was foaled would fail to head them now in their desperate onward course. Though Harris and Colonel Raleigh Gilbert are riding like madmen to stop them, their efforts are utterly vain. Nay, had Jove's winged messenger been there, the god himself would never have stopped those nine merciless hounds, as on they sped, like very demons, in pursuit of their prey. In thirty-five minutes the fox, as bright as a new guinea when he first broke cover, but now beaten and begrimed with soil, bites the dust and is torn into a hundred tatters of brown.

'But what of Russell? On bringing back the hounds to Helland Wood there they found him, sticking to his fox, like the Old Man of the Sea to Sinbad the Sailor; and driving him like wildfire through that great cover, as if it were no bigger than a willow-spinney. Russell greeted the nine hounds thrown in at head and they killed him in an hour and twenty minutes.

'On counting the hounds it was found that three of them were missing; and then came tidings that a third fox had slipped away, and that three hounds had been seen by a turf-cutter near the Jamaica Inn, streaming away towards Brownwilly. The kennel man to Mr Pomeroy Gilbert was then dispatched after them; and, on approaching a tor of that wild moor, he heard the three hounds beneath it, marking among the cavernous rocks that lay at its base. In went the terriers and the kennelman brought him back in great triumph to Bodmin Priory kennels [Pomeroy Gilbert's residence].'

Between Iddesleigh and these Cornish covers lay the lands of John Morth Woolcombe, the Squire of Ashbury for sixty-four years. Ashbury is best approached in a thunderstorm or in a winter's gale. Suddenly in the sub Dartmoor loneliness appears the tower of a church on the skyline. It took two disasters to destroy Ashbury. There was a fire in 1877 and, when the estates were sold up in 1934, the house, rebuilt in Victorian Elizabethan could find no buyer and it was dynamited. Only the enormous walls of the enclosed gardens remain, two 70 yard squares connected by an impressive arch, to remind the occasional visitor of the glories of the House of Woolcombe. John Morth Woolcombe also owned the covers of Broadbury which gave Russell some memorable runs.

But all good things come to an end and by 1830 Russell's kingdom, stretching over the vast moors of East Cornwall and West Devon was breaking up. As fox hunting became more and more popular and foxes were preserved rather than exterminated on sight as vermin, no one pack could adequately hunt that great area. At some time around 1830 the trustees of the Molesworth estate invited Tom Phillips to develop his pack and they built larger kennels at Landue for him. When the Molesworth heir came of age Russell was an honoured guest at someone else's hunting, rather than the MFH, as the Mine-shaft story shows. But he and Phillips remained the best of friends.

That was not the case as far as Russell and Woolcombe were concerned. In a letter to Davies Russell later told the story of their breach in words he deemed suitable for publication. After the division of hunting territory Woolcombe hesitated whether to go in with Phillips or with Russell. Eventually using the inappropriateness of a clergyman being an MFH, the Woolcombes offered to buy Russell's pack and take over his country. The offer and its refusal created bad blood, made worse by Woolcombe becoming a confirmed vulpicide in the 1830s.

From Russell's diary this can be dated to 1831-2. 'December 2nd [1831]. Found a fox in Rutleigh wood [near Ashbury], killed him in the alder bed in five minutes, ditto having been shot at – a bad business'. The entry for February 4th, 1832 is quite explicit: 'Met at Gribbleford Bridge and drew blank in consequence of Woolcombe's bad conduct'. Woolcombe became a decided vulpicide, i.e. his gamekeepers shot foxes, probably in the interests of the pheasants.

Russell's Iddesleigh chapter ended where it had begun – over the rolling farmlands near his parsonage. The week beginning December 5th 1831, was almost the last he spent there uninterrupted by the imminent move to Swimbridge. 'Monday. Found a fox in Halsdon Wood, ran him to a drain in Huish Meadow in one hour and six minutes without a check, bolted him and killed him in Huish Lawn in seven minutes. Cottager.
Wednesday. Mr Arnold's hunting meeting Nethercot. Killed two brace of hares, three Mr A, one to the Governor [his father]. Billy.
Thursday. Bought "Wrestler" of White for Tom Carew.
Friday. Caleb Heale's hunting morning. Killed a leash of hares, one Caleb Heale, one Pomeroy Gilbert. Self one. Billy.
Saturday. Took the hounds to Bydown [near Dennington] and returned home again. Geo Ley came Dec 1st and James Landon Monday 5th. Both returned with me and dined at Dennington.' Although the geographical setting is the same as in 1827 the quarry is more often foxes and there is a clear Monday, Wednesday, Friday pattern to the week's hunting.

One facet of these Iddesleigh years is the enormous endurance Russell had as a rider. For example on March 5th, 1828, a Saturday, he awoke at Landue, hunted with Phillips and had three good runs. Then he set off homewards and slept the night at Iddesleigh to be in church the next morning. The distance from Landue to Iddesleigh is perhaps 35 miles. On September 23rd 1831, he breakfasted with Pomeroy Gilbert at Bodmin, dined at Iddesleigh and then took his hounds on to his Swimbridge home Tordown, a total distance of at least 60 miles. The previous Monday he had left Swimbridge at 7 a.m. and dined at Bodmin at 3 p.m, doing that journey of 60 miles in only eight hours. His longest day may have been October 10th 1831, when he left Haccombe on the Teign estuary in South Devon and went to Calstock, returning the same day, a round trip of 80 miles.

A few runs described in the privacy of his diary give the flavour of the man and the age. Runs were surprisingly long, the land without wire or the dangerous spikes of slashed hedges. 'Saturday, 19th February [1828]. Met the cry from Dennington at Beaford, found a varmint in Pit Brake, ran him to Roborough and back to Beaford and Beaford Moor to

Ring's Ash where Mr Fellowes' hounds joined us, fresh found him opposite Colleton and killed him in Babbage's Brake under Ring's Ash – a brilliant thing!!!' A calendar month later 'Drew Northleigh etc for a fox, did not find – ran a hare towards Gribbleford and killed her. Drew Rutleigh beacon and found Charley immediately – going away in view – to cleave Passaford and Totleigh where we fresh found him – back to Lewdown – Hatherleigh town, Lewer, across the water to Heale, down the bottom to Friar's Hele – where the hounds viewed him into the earths – a most brilliant run!!' On February 14th 1832 'Met my hounds at Eggesford from Crediton [where he had spent the night with his father after taking his wife to Exeter]. A fox stole away from Afton Plantation, which we ran through twelve parishes and took off the hounds at half past six o'clock at Petrockstow – the hounds ran over at least 40 miles of ground – many horses knocked up. Cottager among the numbers - the fox ran through Iddesleigh lawn.' This run was probably part of a Chulmleigh Club Week as Raleigh Gilbert [St Hubert's Hall motto 'Virtute Fortuna Comes'] was staying with Russell and Sir Walter Carew of Haccombe ['Anima non Astutia'] and Paul Treby ['Gaudet Equis et Canibus'] had their hounds in the area.

At the end of each hunting entry between September 1831 and March 1832 Russell noted the name of his mount. During that time he rode ten different horses. As his pocket certainly did not run to such a generous establishment many of them were either on loan or he was trying them out for prospective purchasers. The core of his stable were Cottager and Billy. Cottager he rode 43 times in the winter's season and Billy 33 times. Sadly this was to be Billy's last season. 'On February 27th found a fox in Cleave Coppice, ran him to Ashbury, Narracott and back to Passaford, a ring of one hour and a quarter, when they changed on a fresh fox, which went over the same ground, going from Durden Crosss to Norley Wood, where they fresh found him and, after a most distressing run of two hours they killed him in Burdon Brake near the Golden Inn. The hounds were running five hours without intermission. Billy, poor fellow! I fear he is ruined – he has been a good servant and will be taken care of.' Billy was a fourteen hand bay, part Exmoor, and Russell always claimed he was the best he ever owned. After the pony died, Russell ordered that Billy's skin be used to cover an armchair. Cottager too was eventually used to cover another chair, as was Monkey, a horse that Arthur Harris mentions as belonging to this period. Both horses were extremely temperamental and Cottager was also extremely vicious, its habit being to attempt to bite its rider's foot. Like Facey Romford and Lucy Glitters, Russell knew his horseflesh and was prepared to back his riding ability to make use of lively horses, that because of viciousnesses, could be bought cheap.

Monkey, Cottager and Billy all became armchairs at Tordown, his Swimbridge home. Russell did not explain why he moved there from Iddesleigh to take up the Perpetual Curacy of Swimbridge and Landkey. The living, worth less than £200 a year, was not financially attractive, but was in the gift of the Chichester nexus. Russell was almost certainly living well beyond his means and the influence of his mother-in-law must be suspected, especially as the move was accompanied by the dispersal of his pack. He started using Tordown as a kennel in September 1831. In 1831 the property, inconveniently placed for a working clergyman 2 miles from and 500 feet above Swimbridge, according to Otter Davies was the property of Charles Chichester, a cousin of Penelope's, but the Tithe Award of 1845 states it belonged to John Nott of Bydown. In December he 'took the fixtures' and in April 1832 he moved in with Penelope and Richard Bury. 'Monday, April 8th. Read prayers at Iddesleigh for the last time. W. Love [the new curate] preached! Friday 13th Left Iddesleigh!!!!!! and took the hounds to Tordown – dined and slept at Dennington. Saturday. Went to Tordown!!!! Sunday. Entered my duties at Swimbridge and they "taken" to be arduous!'

So arduous were the duties that he hunted on the Monday and Wednesday of Holy Week and on four days during the week after Easter. But that was in the nature of a final fling as the two last entries of this diary were 'Monday April 30th. Took the hounds to Iddesleigh where I met Tom Hext and Beal, dined at Nethercot, slept at Park. Tuesday. Beal took five couple of my hounds to Haccombe, Tom Hext took eleven couple to Bodmin – both lots to be returned to me whenever I demand them!'

This move to Swimbridge, in the gift of Dean Langdon, a Chichester connection, the use of Tordown, perhaps a Chichester property and the dispersal of his pack all point to one thing: he was out of funds and this threw him on mother-in-law's bounty and control. The spiritual needs of the more numerous populations of Swimbridge and Landkey would take his mind off the expensive nonsense of the hunting field and he would cease to be a prodigal and ne'er-do-well son-in-law. Probably Penelope supported her mother. Iddesleigh must have been a desert for one who had enjoyed Bath in the winter and who was used to having Barnstaple and her numerous Chichester relations within reach. I bet neither she nor her mother knew that there was a 'gentleman's agreement' that Russell could get his hounds back at will.

For Russell the move to Swimbridge was reluctant. He had been very happy at Iddesleigh.

Chapter Seven

EMBATTLED AT SWIMBRIDGE

When Russell and his family moved to Tordown he was given an enormous reception, probably indicating the importance of the Chichesters and Russell's fame as a 'Sportsman'. The *North Devon Journal* wrote on May 31st, 1833. 'The appointment of the Reverend John Russell to the perpetual curacy of Landkey and Swimbridge has given great satisfaction to nearly the whole population. On Wednesday last this event was celebrated by a public holiday. The morning was ushered in by the ringing of bells, which continued the greater part of the day. Friend greeted friend with eyes beaming with gladness. A large party was entertained at Dennington, the paternal seat of the amiable lady of that worthy divine, by whom the earnest wishes for their health and happiness were expressed.

'On the following day the female part of the population of Swimbridge were invited to take tea in the churchyard, where nearly 200 females of all ages sat down to partake of their favourite beverage, provided by their respected clergyman, for whom no doubt the choicest benedictions of heaven were involved'.

Given Russell's career so far this reception was perhaps extravagant. The *Journal* followed his progress. In August he won a saddle at the Swimbridge Races, in September he preached in aid of the Barnstaple Blue Coat School 'in a tone and with a pathos calculated to express fervent feelings of devotion'. His text was Matthew ch 18, verse 14. In July 1834 the paper had an article ' An elegant salver is on display in the window of Mr Mallett, silversmith of Barnstaple. It is inscribed "In testimony of their gratitude and esteem for the kind and faithful services, this tribute, raised by subscription among his parishioners, as a mark of personal attachment was presented on July 8th 1834 to the Reverend

John Russell, who, during the time he has had the care of the parishes of Landkey and Swimbridge, has displayed all the amiable qualities that can adorn a man, both in his public and private capacity. It is the earnest wish of the subscribers that the enduring tie that now binds them may be continued to the latest period of their existence"'.

This press coverage reflects two things. Firstly, rather like Princess Diana, Russell had some sort of star quality and, secondly, that the Journal was a Liberal news sheet. That a Liberal news sheet should give fulsome coverage to a Church of England clergyman, son of the notorious Tory Russell of Crediton needs explanation. Admiral Bury had been `a decided Whig and after 1815 he had always worked for the election of his neighbour Viscount Ebrington, the heir of Earl Fortescue of Filleigh, the major territorial power in the area. The Admiral's elder daughter, Lucy, had married Stephen Bencraft, who had taken over his banking interests in Barnstaple and was a leading Liberal of the town. The Chichesters in North Devon at this period were also staunchly Liberal, as was Russell's hunting friend the Honourable Newton Fellowes of Eggesford. Willy nilly Jack Russell, in the heated atmosphere of the early 1830s, had to be a Liberal too.

And in Barnstaple things had become very hot. The bitterest politics were over the North Devon Infirmary. This laudable institution had been founded in the 1820s by public subscription to provide care for the indigent sick. At its inaugural dinner in January 1825 one of the toasts had been to Admiral Bury and at the church service to bless the new institution a collection was taken at the four church doors by the following ladies; Lady Ebrington, Lady Chichester, Countess Fortescue and Miss Bury [Penelope], proof, if any were still needed of how well Jack had married. This dinner was one of the last the old Admiral attended as in April the *Journal* reported his demise and described his funeral attended by Viscount Ebrington, 13 carriages of mourners plus 'yeomanry and tenantry'. An institution that brought people together in fund raising for a good cause soon turned sour. In 1830 a new physician was needed as the constitution specified two should attend the Infirmary. Appointed in 1825 had been Dr Bignell and Dr Morgan, but Dr Morgan had left town in 1828 and, although promising to return, had not yet done so. The Governors resolved to appoint a Dr Britton and on December 8th 1831 the *Journal* carried a letter signed by Stephen Bencraft supporting Dr Britton and a letter by Dr Britton accepting the post.

Then hell broke loose. The other doctors of the town objected intemperately. The *Journal* of December 15th had a further letter from Bencraft supporting Dr Britton and a letter from Britton which referred to 'most unworthy opposition on the part of the Medical Officers of the establishment' and offered to put his claim to professional proficiency to arbitration. The burden of the medical doctors opposition to Britton was that he was a 'horse-doctor'. Pouring petrol on the flames the *Journal* carried an editorial on December 22nd calling for the acceptance of Britton and an end to 'the narrow selfishness of private interest and party feeling'. On December 19th the *Journal* gave over a whole page to an account of meeting of the North Devon Infirmary, 'attended by most of the contributors'. At that meeting Stephen Bencraft led off. First he recapitulated the recent past, the appointment of Britton the previous March, the united protest of the doctors, who threatened to resign en masse, the order from Lord Ebrington that Britton's credentials be looked into. Bencraft used phrases such as 'prostitute the Infirmary to the professional quarrels of its officers' and 'cruel calumnies and false-hoods have been so industriously and widely circulated'. Later in the meeting Bencraft again rose to confirm his statements about the slanders that had been circulated against Britton and at one point he attempted a vigorous cross questioning of one of the doctors present, Dr Cutcliffe, but was prevented. But he did read out Britton's c.v. From 1793-1803 Britton had studied under Dr Peell, an Edinbrugh educated Bristol surgeon, under whom and other Bristol professors he had studied comparative anatomy. He had also studied chemistry under Sir Humphrey Davy. He had finished his training under Mr Abernethy at St Bartholemew's, London. What perhaps gave rise to rumour was that Peell later opened a 'veterinary establishment'. Britton joined the navy as an assistant surgeon in 1803. In the year of peace in 1804 he took his surgeon's exams and rejoined the navy in 1805 and was posted to the *Victory*, serving at Trafalgar under the chief surgeon, Sir William Beatty. In March 1806 both Beatty and Captain Hardy recommended Britton for promotion, which he received and served with the Navy until 1814. After a period of retraining at St Bartholemew's Britton married a clergyman's daughter and set up a practice in Bristol, which was worth £1000 a year when he sold it. Perhaps Bencraft's warmth on his behalf may have been due to the naval connection: Britton was the Bury nominee, or, as Bencraft put it Britton was 'a man, whose public services alone in the cockpit of the *Victory* entitled him to the gratitude and respect of every true born Englishman' . The meeting confirmed Britton's appointment by 43 votes to 33. After the meeting Viscount Ebrington is reported to have told the medical men to 'go to your houses and dissect horses, cats and other beasts in order to arrive at the same ability as Dr Britton has already attained'.

Immediately there was schism. Drs Bignell, Copner, Cutcliffe, Hiern, Harding and Winter immediately resigned and their vacant positions were advertised. Sir Bourchier Wrey of Tawstock led a group of sub-scribers to form the Barnstaple and North Devon Dispensary. A leading Barnstaple figure, Richard Bremridge had been in London and had missed the big meeting. On his return he had words with Law, one of Bencraft's banking partners, threatening the possibility of the resigning doctors refusing to accept the notes of the bank led by Pike, Law and Bencraft. Later he denied saying that there was a group who would organise a run on the bank that would drive Bencraft out of town. On the morning of December 31st Bremridge wrote the following in the Infirmary Visitors' Book : ' I have this day struck out my name from the House committee list as I could not consent to remain on the Committee after the disgraceful and insulting treatment the late medical depart-ment had received from some of the subscribers and Committee men with whom I had been acting'. On January 2nd Bencraft met Bremridge in the street, but the latter avoided conversation. However on January 4th Bremridge had to cash a cheque In Gribble's Bank where he encoun-tered Bencraft and the dialogue went as follows:

Bencraft: ' Did you mean that entry at me?'

Bremridge: ' I will answer no questions. You may take it as you like'

Bencraft: 'You dirty blackguard, did you mean it at me? if you did you damned blackguard I will break every bone in your skin.'

At this point Mr Gribble came round the counter and placed himself between the two men and Bencraft struck Bremridge in the face, throw-ing the punch over Gribble's shoulder and another partner took Bencraft away. As he went Bencraft shouted 'You coward, you were afraid to come to the Committee Room yesterday,- if you had I would have kicked you out'.

After this Bremridge went to his friends Captain Grace and Mr Westbrook, presumably to arrange a duel as the Mayor immediately summoned him and bound him over to keep the peace. Bremridge went straight to the law and the matter came up as a *Nisi Prius* suit in the March Exeter Assizes. Naturally a large number of local people, includ-ing Russell, attended the court. The proceedings did not go to the wire as Follett, Bencraft's attorney offered reparation and in court Bencraft offered Bremridge his hand, which in spite of the Judge's request Bremridge totally refused to grasp. In the obituary that appeared in the *Journal* when Bremridge died in June 1878 it was reported that he had said 'I would rather meet a mad dog than a Reformer' and that 'it was not in his nature to do things by halves.'

Then there began a subscription war between the Infirmary and the Dispensary. In September 1832, before he took up residence in Swimbridge, Russell was reported in the *Journal* as contributing £2-2s-

0d to the Infirmary and for the rest of his life he was a regular fund-raising preacher for the Infirmary. For example in March 1841 he collected £11-7s-0d after a sermon in Swimbridge and Sleeman, his curate, collected £12-10s-0d in Landkey. Whig-Liberals supported the Infirmary and Tories the Dispensary.

And the extraordinary bitterness of the clash between Bencraft and Bremridge is due to the awful tensions between Whigs and Tories in Barnstaple in the years of the Reform Bill crisis. In September 1831, Bremridge, then Mayor, declined to chair a meeting called to demand reform. In his absence Gribble had taken the chair and Bencraft had proposed a fierce resolution against 'influence, corruption and electoral abuses.' In October in another meeting Gribble proposed and Bencraft seconded a resolution calling upon William IV to create enough peers to overcome the Tory majority against Parliamentary Reform in the Lords. After the passage of the Reform Bill Bencraft was active both in the campaign for J.P.B. Chichester, who stood as the Reform candidate in Barnstaple, and in the campaign of Viscount Ebrington, who stood with Newton Fellowes for the new electoral district of North Devon. In Barnstaple Chichester was successful, but the other successful candidate, a Major Fancourt, seems to have bribed his way in and the call among Barnstaple Liberals for the next twenty years was for 'purity of election'. In spite of the wider franchise Tories could succeed as many of the still limited electorate would sell their votes for about £6 and beer. The whole scandal was exploded in 1852 with a petition against the result of the previous election, which had resulted in the election of two Tories Sir William Fraser and Richard Bremridge and the defeat of Viscount Ebrington [the son of the candidate of 1832]. In the ensuing Inquiry Stephen Bencraft's sons, Russell's nephews Lionel and Incledon, were active on the Liberal side and the Bremridges for the Tories.

As Perpetual Curate of Swimbridge cum Landkey Russell may only have been on the fringes of these Barnstaple events. But as the husband of Lucy Bencraft's younger sister he would have been implicated by association. Swimbridge was a large parish and its politics were complicated. Unusually there were four major landowners. Penelope's cousin Richard Chichester of Hall in the neighbouring parish of Tawstock, owned 1000 acres, Lord Rolle 750 acres, the Duke of Bedford and John Nott 900 acres each, while the landowner whose local influence was perhaps strongest in the area as a whole rather than the parish in particular, Earl Fortescue, owned only 60 acres. Of these major landowners only John Nott lived in the parish and his house at Bydown was very close to Russell's mother-in-law's residence at Dennington. In

1845 at the time of the Tithe Award he also owned Tordown, while Dennington was stated to be in the ownership of the Duke of Bedford. Both these 'facts' are surprising. All previous accounts state that Tordown House was owned by Chichester and the presumption was that the Burys owned Dennington. John Nott also had the lease of the tithes, which he collected on behalf of the Dean and Chapter of Exeter Cathedral.

Nott seems to have been a difficult, even cantankerous character. He was certainly unpopular. In 1830 southern England was disturbed by the 'Captain Swing' Riots, a movement of the hungry rural poor in demand of higher wages and a reduction in rents and tithes. Devon generally was more peaceful than counties further east, but there was quite serious unrest in Swimbridge which was directed against John Nott. Around Christmas 1830 a group of angry labourers besieged Bydown on at least two occasions to demand higher wages and a reduction in tithes and rents. The unrest ended with a potentially dangerous encounter on Kerscott Hill between the mob and Lord Ebrington, who managed to defuse the situation. Later the ringleaders were arrested and put before the Assizes in Exeter.

Probably Nott took an almost immediate dislike to Russell, the man with a talent for unpopularity being galled by the man with a talent for getting on with all and sundry, and certainly who outshone him within the parish. Probably Nott was a Tory. Certainly the glee with which the Liberal *Journal* recounted Nott's troubles implies that he was no reformer, and, as we shall see, he had no objections to colluding with Bishop Phillpotts, probably the most reactionary bishop on the bench. In 1840 hostilities between Parson Russell and Squire Nott became quite absurd. It seems that in October 1840 Nott went to Exeter to see the Bishop with a farrago of accusations against Russell – that he hunted excessively to the point of neglecting duty, that he took part in horse-racing and that he gambled and behaved in other ways unsuited to a clergyman of the Church of England. Phillpotts eagerly saw a chance of disciplining one of his clergy of whom he had come to disapprove, one closely connected with the leading Radical of Barnstaple, Stephen Bencraft, one who was a friend of those Chichester, Fortescue and Newton Fellowes Members of Parliament who were his Westminster opponents. In fact Phillpotts later admitted that Russell had come to see him and had warned him that Nott was going to bring accusations and had asked to speak to his bishop about them. In defiance of all good pastoral custom Phillpotts had refused to listen to Russell, who I guess was going to warn his bishop that Nott had become deranged with spite.

Phillpotts knew the ways of the courts and told Nott to get some effective evidence. Nott was especially smarting over some verses against him, circulating in the neighbourhood, whose author he thought was Russell. He was also angry at remarks he thought Russell had made at a Vestry Meeting which alleged that Squire Nott would not help the poor. This was a particularly touchy subject as in May 1841 Nott was summonsed for non-payment of Poor Rates to the tune of £24-6s-8d and the Court issued a Distress Warrant on his goods to that amount. Delays in the law probably meant that this non-payment of Poor Rates had happened in early 1840 and was behind Russell's comments about Nott's attitude to the poor.

Anyway on November 6th 1840 Nott, Russell and Sleeman met the Bishop, who had fixed the appointment and who had invited Sleeman to accompany Russell. Nott had collected his evidence, but he was a J.P. and should have known his law and it should be remembered that the Tolpuddle Martyrs had been convicted on the grounds of taking and administering illegal oaths. He acted upon rumours of odd goings on at a party given by Mrs Eastman, a close friend of the Russells at Yelland House, where rumour had it Russell had indulged in some gambling. To get his evidence Nott had summoned some of Mrs Eastman's servants to Bydown. One of them Thomas Huxtable, aged sixteen, stated that he had seen Russell at a large party play 'thimble-rigging' and that he had won two shillings at it and that sixpence of those winnings fell behind a chair and that Russell had said that if he could find it he could have it. Another of Nott's witnesses, Ann Burrow, stated that a child died the Friday before Christmas and was not buried until the Friday after Christmas. Another, Grace Short complained that, during her husband's long final illness, Russell only visited once, but that Mr Lovering, the Baptist minister, came and prayed over him. Nott had made the mistake of taking this evidence 'on oath' and making them all swear on the Good Book. Phillpotts knew his law and shied away, especially as Ann Burrow said she had absolutely no complaint to make about the baby's burial. He went onto another tack and attacked Russell and Sleeman as hunting men. Tradition has it that Russell, politely told him to mind his own business and, as Russell had his parson's freehold, there was nothing that could be done against him. But Phillpotts could revoke Sleeman's licence, which he did. Whereupon Russell pointed out the problem of running two large parishes without a curate, hence Phillpotts postponed the revocation of licence until 'next year'.

The next stage in the story can only be explained by Nott's being blinded by rage. For some reason he wrote to Sleeman's father, or perhaps Sleeman's father wrote angrily to Nott as the cause of his son's loss of licence and Nott replied intemperately. At any rate in the letter he wrote to Sleeman's father Nott gave opportunity for Russell to sue for libel. The case came up at Exeter in March 1841 and, to add to the excitement, Bishop Phillpotts was subpoenaed to give evidence. As the *North Devon Journal* put it on the 16th 'we should ourselves have had the pleasure of gratifying the eager expectations of our readers. No trial for many years has excited so much interest in the neighbourhood'. But expectations had to be postponed. Pleading a key debate in the House of Lords, Phillpotts asked for a postponement and the trial had to be reported in the issue of March 23rd. In court Russell's lawyer asserted that Russell had had no part in composing or circulating the verses about Nott. Secondly on the matter of what he had said in the Vestry meeting, Russell stated that 'it had been made in accordance with Mr Russell's understanding of the message which he had received from Mr Nott. If that was not in accordance with what Mr Nott had meant, he, Mr Russell, offered his apology'. Nott recognised the inevitable, accepted Russell's 'apology' and himself apologised for any imputations on Mr Russell's character he may have written. Russell was awarded costs of £200. Game, set and, as we shall see, match. The Bishop meanwhile had come down from London and was waiting across the way in the Palace to give the evidence that, as it happened, was not required.

Russell's ride back to Swimbridge was in the nature of a triumphal procession. Whatever route he took he had to go through his old parish of South Molton. The *Journal* reported the ' the Reverend gentleman was greeted on all hands by the warm congratulations of his friends and on his return through South Molton the bells were ringing merrily and numbers of the most respectable inhabitants crowded round him to express their gratification at the successful termination of the suit. The bells of Swimbridge were not rung, Mr Russell having given peremptory prohibition of any demonstration which might offend the feelings of the defeated'. The report in the Tory *Advertiser* was much more restrained, giving no advanced notice of the case, having the barest bones of a report, not mentioning the damages nor the bells of South Molton. Perhaps this confirms the Toryism of Nott and the Liberal associations of Russell in the 1830s and 1840s.

The matter did not end there. In May 1841 Nott, a J.P himself, was summonsed for non payment of rates to the tune of £24-6s-8d. The court gave the Overseers of the Poor a distress warrant for the sum against Nott's property. In June Nott boiled over and wrote a most impolitic letter to the Editor of the *Journal*, which was published on June 8th claiming that Russell had been spreading rumours that Nott had not paid over the moneys awarded in the Russell v Nott case. Nott started by quoting letters of March 1841 showing that the money had been paid. He quoted a report that, as late as May 31st Russell had been saying the moneys had not been paid. The letter concluded: 'When a subscription was proposed some time since for the poor of Swimbridge, I sent a message to Mr Russell to acquaint him that I would contribute £5; and, although he acknowledged that he had received the message, he afterwards, at a public meeting of parishioners stated that I would not subscribe – that I did not approve of it!! – Mr Russell has since admitted the truth of this, but says that he made such statement under a erroneous apprehension. Mr Russell seems to have laboured under a similar erroneous impression as to the alleged non-payment of the £200, as well as on other matters; and though it may be hoped that it happens more by accident than design, it is, to say the least of it, rather singular that none of Mr Russell's erroneous impressions should ever be at all in my favour. If, however from the respect due to the assertion of a clergyman, it be conceded, (difficult and incomprehensible as it seems, under all the circumstances, to imagine such a thing) that Mr Russell had not by any means been brought acquainted with the payment of the £200, still I may ask, whether he was justified, without first ascertaining the fact from his solicitor, in so positively asserting the money had not been paid! and whether his intent was 'wicked' or 'charitable' in so doing. And as I refer to the assertion made by Mr Russell on the 31st May, of the money not having been paid up to the preceding Saturday, that he must have had some recent information on the subject as to enable him to speak particularly as to that day, I beg to ask from whom he had that information? or what grounds had he for making that assertion?

Mr Russell and his Solicitor having had the option of offering their own explanation through the public press, and having declined to do so, I trust I shall not have been considered as acting improperly in publishing this statement of the facts, in contradiction to a false report too widely circulated to be sufficiently met through any less public channel.

I am, Sir, your obedient Servant, John Nott, Bydown, June 8th, 1841.'

A letter best ignored.

In June 1841 Nott must have known he was in serious trouble. Mrs Eastman, who had appeared in Russell's diary as early as 1825 as a family friend of the Burys, was furious at the suborning of her servants by Nott the previous October. In interviewing those servants he had forced them to take an oath as to the accuracy of their testimony. As a J.P. he should have known that administering an oath on such an occasion was illegal and expressly contrary to a recent statute designed to prevent the growth of trade unions and other potentially revolutionary

The Honourable Mark Rolle, from a painting in Lord Clinton's collection.

Stevenstone, the impossibly grand house built by Mark Rolle and pulled down in less than a hundred years. (DRO)

Her two boys as cadets at Britannia, where Russell visited them. Prince Albert and Prince George, later George V. (From the Royal Archives)

Alexandra, Princess of Wales, an especial favourite of Russell's and described in one of his letters as a 'lovely little creature'. (From the Royal Archives)

Dunster castle, the home of Russell's Luttrell friends, where he and his father often stayed and where the Prince of Wales stayed on his hunting trip to Exmoor in 1879. (Somerset RO)

An oil painting of Jack Russell surrounded by his hounds. Russell was about fifty years old when this was painted. Note the 'Jack Russell' terrier under the horse. A painting donated to Blundell's School by F.W.B. Smythe.

'Snoopy', a Jack Russell of the working type, belonging to the Countess of Arran, photographed in front of Castle Hill. (Taken by A.C.D. Noon)

Jack Russell in vigorous older age, smiling.
No wonder he was a favourite with the ladies.

Jack Russell in sterner mood.

'The Poltimore Hunt', a painting presented to Lord Poltimore in 1860 showing Lord Poltimore leading the field across country north of Exeter. Killerton is in the background. Russell is the rider in clerical black immediately behind his Lordship. An oil by Widgery in the possession of Sir Hugh Stucley. (Taken by S. Goodwin)

Russell in old age at the front door of Dennington in the last years before he moved back to Tordown. (Lent by Sir Hugh Stucley)

Tordown, Russell's first and last Swimbridge home. (Taken by A.C.D. Noon)

Black Torrington Rectory where Russell died in 1883, aged eighty seven.
The 'extension' on the right would not have been there in his day. The tower of his
last church, St Mary's, can be seen behind the Rectory. (The Beaford Archive)

organisations. The Tolpuddle Martyrs had been convicted under its provisions, and Mrs Eastman took up the cudgels and instigated a prosecution of Nott under its provisions. Everyone always denied that Russell had put her up to it. In early August the County was treated to the spectacle of a Bill of Indictment being drawn up against a landowner and J.P. who would be prosecuted as a criminal in the Lent Assizes of 1842.

In March 1842 the case of Regina v Nott commenced. The *Journal* announced unctuously 'We shall not go into the details of this unfortunate case for we very much regret the distraction which the parish of Swimbridge has been too long subject on account of it. We earnestly desire a restoration of peace and good neighbourliness which are essential to the comfort of the parishioners and indispensable to the interests of religion, which are seriously involved and have suffered severely from the disruption.' Of course the *Journal* proceeded to report the case fully. The evidence of the servants clearly established that Nott had administered 'illegal' oaths on at least three occasions in his pursuit of 'dirt', so that he could provide Phillpotts with ammunition to discipline Russell. Both Phillpotts and Archdeacon Barnes were summoned to give evidence of the meetings in the previous autumn. Phillpotts' testimony was that he had not seen Nott's evidence before the meeting on November 6th, 1840, that as soon as he saw the evidence Nott had produced, he thought it was illegally acquired and promptly closed the case. He claimed somewhat ingenuously that he had not suspended Sleeman, and he chose his words rather too nicely when he averred that he had expressed 'a strong opinion on hunting in an aggravated form'. He added 'If any complaint had come from any quarter deserving credit that a curate was a fox-hunter, I should have thought it my duty, if found true, to revoke his licence.' This episcopal evidence was not really relevant to the case and one supposes that the lawyers were allowed to tease an unpopular bishop. Nott was found guilty and sentenced to one month's imprisonment. Nott did not go to jail. In May 1842 Nott was granted a 'rule nisi' and a fresh trial. Nott and the bishop having been humiliated Mrs Eastman dropped her charges. Nevertheless victory to the Russell and Eastman camp.

Russell must have been in the best of spirits to enjoy the joyous festivities of June 28th, 1842. The Mayor of Barnstaple for the year was a wealthy merchant, Gilbert Knill Cotton, who was a friend of the Russells and Bencrafts. In 1828 Russell had come to Swimbridge, while yet the Curate of Iddesleigh, expressly to officiate at the wedding of Gilbert Knill Cotton and Mary Ann Burden, and in August 1834 he had baptised their daughter also called Mary, who in 1866 was to marry the

Russell's only surviving child, Richard Bury Russell. The mayor had organised an enormous river picnic in honour of the fifth anniversary of the coronation of Queen Victoria. The day began with church bells and the discharge of cannon. At 8.30 the company boarded their vessels, which, according to the press, numbered more than fifty sail and they included a 'musical barge' weighed down with fifty musicians. The armada sailed to the junction of the Taw and Torridge where they were joined by a flotilla from Bideford. The whole body than picnicked on Braunton Sands, except the select company on the Mayor's Barge who dined aboard at three o'clock, then still the normal hour for that meal. Jack Russell sat on the Mayor's right hand and replied to the toast of 'The Clergy'. It was a perfect day of sun and zephyrs and the boats returned to Barnstaple on the evening tide to the strains of the musical barge.

This series of skirmishes with Nott and Phillpotts was not Russell's only brush with the Law. A diary entry for March 19th 1844 runs 'I took the hounds out and I was subpoenaed to attend the Assizes at Exeter!' He had sufficient sangfroid to continue the meet. The *North Devon Journal* reported later that 'We are happy to find that the actions which were entered for trial are compounded, Russell v Arnold.' But it is not known what that fuss was about. There was a family of landowners in Iddesleigh called Arnold so it may have been some property dispute there.

Russell also took part in other ceremonials of the North Devon country. It was an age interested in agricultural improvement and the week before the Mayor's Maritime Picnic Russell had attended a meeting and dinner of the Barnstaple and North Devon Agricultural Society. In October 1842, at the dinner of the Chittlehampton and Warkleigh Agricultural Society he was on the top table and proposed a toast to 'Lord Clinton and Mr Drake, the Trustees of the property of Lord Rolle' and later a toast to 'the Prosperity of the Chittlehampton and Warkleigh Agricultural Society'. By modern standards this would have been a heavy dinner. In total their were nine toasts – Jack Russell's two and the following: 'The Queen, her Sex's Pride, her Country's Glory', 'Albert, Prince of Wales', 'Prince Albert and the rest of the Royal Family', 'the Army and Navy', 'Earl Fortescue', 'Mark Trefusis Clinton' [the heir of the Rolles], and 'the Clergy of the Diocese'. Nine Toasts, nine speeches, a long menu and the pre- and post-toast drinking, but the horses knew the way home. The press also reported his taking part in other agricultural societies' meetings, for example the North Molton and Twitchen. There is no evidence that he was interested in agricultural techniques, but these societies were part of the fabric of rural life and the prosperity of agriculture determined the livelihood of his parishioners. He had every right to be there, he was popular and part of the attraction of the occasions. At a time when so many clergy of the Church of England were Evangelical or Puseyite and pursuing theological vendettas far removed from the concerns of laymen it was refreshing to see a clergyman, whom even Phillpotts in 1831, in the privacy of his diary, referred to as 'a fine young man, said to be active and useful as a clergyman and a good preacher,' who was 'on their wavelength'.

Russell was also a prominent Freemason. Of course at this date Freemasonry was seen as respectable. He was a Chaplain of the Provincial Grand Lodge at Barnstaple and a Provincial Grand Chaplain. He read the dedication service of the Tiverton Lodge when it opened the new Masonic Hall in 1834. This was a lifelong commitment and when nearly eighty years old he attended the installation of the Prince of Wales at the Albert Hall on St George's Day, 1875. He was also a member of the Barnstaple Turnpike Trust, occasionally an Income Tax Commissioner for the Hundred of South Molton and often appointed to various ad hoc bodies such as a commission to investigate abuses in the Barnstaple Workhouse. He got involved in local mineral exploitation, to the detriment of his pocket. West country mining was enjoying a boom time in the 1840s and in 1844 the Swimbridge Mining Company was set up to prospect for lead and silver. In 1846 this company opened a mine in East Coombe and Penelope Russell 'launched' its water wheel, christening it Mary Ann. He was to the fore in all aspects of local life, but he was not a typical mid century clergyman and this aggravated the zealous, although it pleased his neighbours and most of his parishioners.

Typical of his capacity to aggravate the zealous was his attitude to the Temperance Movement when it came to proselytise in Swimbridge in January 1845. The *Journal* reported that ' the village school was kindly lent by the respected curate the Reverend J. Russell. At the tea which preceded the meeting the Reverend gent's colleague sent his silver tea service with the remark "that teetotallers were worthy of the best things".' In the local press meetings of the Missionary societies and other clerical organisations were well reported, but Russell's name never appears. He would preach a sermon to raise funds for hospitals and schools, but he was not to the fore in issues dear to the heart of his clerical brethren. That did his popularity and influence no harm as far as his unfanatical parishioners were concerned. That he aggravated his bishop and the Notts of this world did not mean he was not a good and useful member of society.

Chapter Eight

HUNTING PARSON

W hat was unremarkable in a young, relatively unknown bachelor curate in the 1820s in the backwoods of South Molton and
Iddesleigh before the coming of Phillpotts, Reform and the
Railway was increasingly a matter of comment as the 1830s became the
1840s and the high tide of Evangelicalism in the 1850s. As told at the end
of the Iddesleigh chapter I suspect that his mother-in-law hoped Jack
had given up his hounds and would now settle down to the 'arduous'
duties of serving the numerous parishioners of Landkey and
Swimbridge. Evidence that he did not do so comes from three sources
the sporting press, the local press and volumes of his diaries that have
been preserved by the descendants of his friend Buck who is first mentioned in those diaries in November 1827, when on Thursday 29th he '
hunted with Buck at Afton, dined and slept there, good sport'. [Afton
being Affeton Castle in East Worlington.] Russell's hunting diaries for
1834-5, 1835-6, 1836-7, 1837-8, 1838-9, 1841-2, 1842-3, 1843-4 all survive
in a single volume kept at Hartland Abbey. A much fuller account of the
season 1845-6 has also been found.

Lying loose within the Hartland Abbey volume is a letter of 21st
February [?] 1870 from Russell to a friend. The seventy-four-year-old
writes from Swimbridge ' .....alas, alas, you have abandoned my dear
old happy hunting grounds and I am not allowed to reoccupy them.
How miserable the loss of my little pack has made me. They were very
good and I could "let them out" morning, noon or evening as it suited
me. But now to meet any hounds I must ride 20 or 30 miles on the road
every day. 'Tis too far for a man of seventy four and if I stop I shall fall
to pieces in six months. I have been laid up for the last six weeks with
whooping cough and am half dead with it – seen no hunting since
Christmas, but hope to meet Portsmouth tomorrow at Ashreigney'. If he
felt like that at seventy-four neither a mother-in-law nor a bishop nor
sanctimonious humbug was going to stop him hunting at thirty-five!

Lack of finance might though. His stipend for Swimbridge and Landkey never reached £200 a year. Records of the sale of Colleton Barton, the valuable Chulmleigh property which he inherited from Mrs Bury, record that he had taken out mortgages of £1000 in 1827, £1000 again in 1829, £1500 in 1841 and £1500 in 1843 and that the proceeds of the sale of that estate in the late 1850s were used to pay them off. Russell's financial position had become so dire by the mid 1840s that Jane Bury redrafted her will, a copy of which has survived, dated January 17th 1845, just before she died. All her property she bequeathed to John Dene of Horwood for him to hold in trust for 'Penelope Russell, the wife of the Reverend John Russell for her sole and separate use … independently of her said husband and so that the same may not be subject or liable to the debts, control, interference or engagements of the said John Russell, her husband … as if she were sole and unmarried. And I appoint my said daughter, Penelope, sole executrix.' In Russell's favour it must be recorded that the reason Jane Bury gave for 'disinheriting' her other daughter Lucy Bencraft was that Lucy had been well provided for by an aunt, Amy Chichester. Jane Bury died in May 1848 and John Russell Senior had predeceased her, dying on a visit to Charles Carpenter of Launceston in March 1847 at the age of eighty-seven. These deaths may have given the Russell coffers a new lease of life, but after the sale of the last of the Colleton estate in 1859 Russell's career as an MFH was effectively over.

The Hartland diaries clearly indicate the extent of Russell's hunting activities in middle life. In the three seasons between September 1834 and April 1837 his fox-hunting took up seventy-three, seventy-four and seventy-three days respectively with a regular three day a week pattern, punctuated by whole weeks or fortnights when two or more packs met for Chulmleigh Club Weeks. The 1838 diary is very brief and just gives the information that '15 brace of foxes were killed'. He hunted his pack on seventy-eight days in 1838-9. In the season of 1841-2 his pack worked on ninety-one days, returning to about seventy days between 1842 and 1845. The very full diary of 1844-5 records that he went fox-hunting on no less than ninety-five days between September 1st and the end of April. The sporting press also refer to his attendance at meets of the Stag Hounds who had two short seasons in August and April and May. Russell only had to endure the 'meatless' months of June and July. In the years not covered by existing diaries one may assume that he also hunted between seventy and one hundred days a season and the occasional press notice indicates that the North Devon Hunt, as Russell's pack was always called (indicative of his need, even in palmy days for the assistance of subscriptions to help with expenses) hunted about five days every fortnight.

However the two seasons missing from the diaries, Sept 1839 to April 1841 may have a more sinister explanation. Cryptic comments in the *Sporting Magazine* refer to a vulpicide on the loose in Russell's territory and 'Rodney' in an article 'Tour of the West' in May 1841 avowed that 30 foxes had been shot in Stoodleigh. In January 1842 there was a further diatribe by 'Brunecheval' against fox killing, especially against fox killing by gin-traps, replete with evidence of foxhounds running into traps and having their pads ripped off. Obviously the culprit was well known to the *Sporting Magazine's* West Country readers and equally clearly he was an owner of wide acres to cause the disruption to Russell's activities. It is in these years that Dulverton hunting fortnights developed in September and in the spring when hunters were treated to Russell's foxhounds and the Staghounds on alternate days. Enthusiastic sporting journalists referred to Dulverton as 'the Melton of the West'. Also in these years an Ivybridge Club Week grew up around the activities of Sir Walter Palk Carew's and Mr Bulteel's hounds and continued for many years.

Another handicap Russell suffered about this time was the loss of Sam, his huntsman and general kennel factotum. In September 1839 the *Sporting Magazine* reported 'Mr Russell, the much respected Master of the Pack [the NDH] has in addition to losing several couple of most valuable hound from some dire malady, experienced a greater loss in his Whipper -in – a truly valued and tried servant. His death was most heart-rending and the circumstances attached most distressing.' Unfortunately the *North Devon Journal* for that year is in too bad a condition to be released to readers and a microfilm has yet to be produced, so the 'distressing' event cannot be discovered.

Before looking at Russell's hunting in these middle years of his life, it might be helpful to get an 'overview' of the history of fox-hunting in Devon. Before Russell's death in 1883 one may distinguish four phases. The first phase was the time before the emergence of George Templer of Stover. As mentioned in previous chapters eighteenth century hunting tended to be long and slow and it was Templer who introduced Meynell-style fast hunting to Devon and Templer's most proficient acolyte was Russell. In this second phase first Templer, until his financial disaster, then increasingly Russell dominated hunting in Devon from his base in Iddesleigh in alliance with Arthur Harris of Stowford and Phillips of Landue. Newton Fellowes of Eggesford might claim to have been a leader of hunting society, but his was too quirky a character to fill the role of MFH properly. In the 1820s and 1830s it was still possible in a Devon isolated from the rest of the country by the lack of railways, for all the hunting bloods to gather at the Chulmleigh Club

Weeks. The third phase, roughly 1835-60, can be seen as evolving from Russell's move to Swimbridge and the break up of his pack. The popularity of hunting lead to the development of more centres and more packs – chiefly Mr Bulteel's at Flete House, whose pack was carried on after his early death by Charles Trelawney at Ivybridge; and Sir Walter Palk Carew's pack at Haccombe, with other kennels at Marley, where those who could endure his company could enjoy sport. In the later 1840s the latter handed his pack to his kinsman Thomas Carew of Colliepriest and they then were called 'The Tiverton Fox Hounds'. Newton Fellowes maintained a pack at Eggesford and lesser packs, such as Mr Archer's, Mr Morgan's and Sir Henry Searle's at Dartmouth filled in the gaps. Towards the end of this period many wealthy Devonians were enabled by the railways to spend the seasons hunting with the 'crack' Midland hunts at Melton or elsewhere. The sporting press were full of their runs over the flat grasslands of Leicestershire, but increasingly sporting journalists became a bit scathing about such hunts which were more akin to thirty minute steeplechases with the fox hunted in full view most of the time. They contrasted the simplicity of Leicestershire hunting with the skill shown by Russell and his hounds in hunting the fox in the difficult lands of Devon, where hounds had to work and men had to ride with much greater skill. As his peers fell away by death, George Templer and Bulteel both died in the 1840s, Newton Fellowes in the 1850s, or like Sir Walter Carew moved to Leicestershire, Russell remained and became more pre-eminent, as long as his money lasted.

The fourth phase may be dated by Russell's retirement as MFH of the North Devon Hunt which coincided with the emergence of three new, young scions of the hunting aristocracy. The young Hon. Mark Rolle developed the Stevenstone Hunt. The young Lord Poltimore who inherited the Poltimore estates in 1855 started the Poltimore pack in 1857. Newton Fellowes died in 1854, having been the fourth Earl of Portsmouth for less than a year, and was succeeded by the quaintly named Isaac Newton Fellowes as fifth Earl, who also showed great interest in hunting and developed the Eggesford pack. All three acknowledged a great debt of gratitude to Russell, who now became a revered elder statesman, and keeping a small 'Cry' of hounds for his own amusement until 1870 when, almost seventy-five years old he gave them up.

Throughout his life from his mid thirties to his early sixties it is clear that Russell hunted his hounds either as owner-Master or as Master of a subscription pack, usually three days a week. A typical fortnight in October 1845 was as follows: 'Monday 13th. New Bridge [5 miles] found a litter in Bude's Bottom, after a little rattling one went away to Chorley, where he turn'd back, and was kill'd where he was found, time one hour and three quarters. Found a second at Brimsworthy Brake and earth'd him near Tawstock House. "Serva".

Thursday 16th. Hacche [6 miles] – found in Holy Victory's Wood, and earth'd in Halse Wood. Found a second in Venn Wood, earth'd, gain'd and kill'd him in Leigh Wood – time No 1 one hour and forty five minutes, No 2 one hour and a quarter. "The Bison".

Saturday 18th. Blatchford Mills. [8 miles]. Drew Mr Dennis's Wood – no fox. Trotted on to Swinnon Hill where Mr and Mrs Frank Hole and daughters were waiting with a "Bag Man"!! which was turned down and soon disposed of. Drew on towards Arlington and found in Wooley Wood, going straight down the covers to Chilpham Bridge – best pace, where he cross'd the river, pointing for Loxhore, but the hounds pressed him so severely that he turn'd right about, cross'd the bottom and over the hill into Southwood, where several foxes were soon on foot, one of which went away to Horsewell with some of the couples after him, which I stopp'd at Whichford Downs about 5 o'clock. "Blackberry".

Tuesday 21st. Eggesford Kennels. [16 miles]. Found at 4 o'clock! in Bridge Bottom, ran a few fields and took them home. N.B. We drew the Winkleigh Covers blank in the morning!! "Serva".

Wednesday 22nd. Yard Down [8 miles]. Found in Molland Wood and ran the covers the whole day, no blood. Lost "Welcome". Mr and Mrs Smyth sent her to me on the following morning. "Blackberry".

Saturday 25th. Romansleigh Village. [12 miles]. Found under Horridge and kill'd at Slashcot in 1 hour and 25 minutes. "Serva".'

Sometimes something occurred to distract him from hunting. Twice in 1845-6 he left his hounds at mid-day in the charge to attend a 'Railway Meeting' – an extension was being planned to Barnstaple and Bury lands at Lapford and Chulmleigh were on one of the possible routes. In December 1845 he became ill and 'confined to my bed and house from the 13th to January 7th, but Parkyn, the Whip kept the fixtures.' In January 1844 he had dashed to Harrow on the rumour of a fever raging in the school to which his only surviving son Bury had been transferred from Blundell's. It was a false alarm so he went to the Tring Steeplechase on the 17th, Baron Rothschilds' Stag Hounds on the 18th and some hounds at Newport Pagnell on the 18th, so that week was not entirely wasted. But usually the diaries report the three day a week pattern, with three or four horses at his disposal, the assistance of a Whip, with meets up to 15 miles away from the kennels in Swimbridge.

The climaxes of each season were the Club Weeks. These were variously held at Chulmleigh, Ivybridge, South Molton and, less formally, at Dulverton. After he moved to Swimbridge Russell attended Chulmleigh Weeks in December 1834, November 1835 and November 1840. There may have been others, but these are the ones verifiable by the press or diaries. On each occasion three packs shared the hunting six days a week for a fortnight: in 1834 the packs were Sir Walter Palk Carew's, the Hon. Newton Fellowes and Russell's; in 1835 Tom Phillips replaced Newton Fellowes, and in 1840 Bulteel of Flete House replaced Phillips. Ivybridge weeks for 1839,1840 and 1850 are recorded, so that November 1840 must have been very busy! In both years the entertainment was provided by Sir Walter and Bulteel. By 1850 Bulteel was dead and his hounds had been taken over by Charles Trelawney and the three packs were Sir Henry Searle's, Trelawney's and Russell's. This Ivybridge Week was covered by the *Sporting Magazine's* journalist who wrote under the nom de plume of 'Gelert'. After praising the apt mix of hunting and riding to be found in Devon as opposed to the crude Midland gallopings, Gelert wrote 'Mr Russell's day was par excellence the day of the week. To him especially pertained the felicity of showing an undeniably good run and of testing the condition of artificial [sic] life, the blood, bone and mettle of the kennel against the stark denizen of the forest – the wild fox of Dartmoor They found him in Overbrent Wood and were quickly aware that the gentleman meant running. He broke away over Woodholes and the pack broke after him as the thunder clap follows the flash. He pounded for Dorkhill ridge and Hayford and led them at a slapping pace over some of the finest grass sward in England. He then crossed the river under Huntingdon Warren and up to Whiteyborough where he turned for Zeal Tor. From this point the short chop notes of the leading hounds became less frequent, death was in the sound and under Shipley Bridge they caught sight of him and killed him in the river. Time fifty-two minutes without the shadow of a check. Those who live in cultivated lands have little conception of the wild scenery over which our western friends revel; grass, old rough grass, sown at the Deluge, is the carpet which Nature has spread for their pastime; every brook has a visible bottom, the broadest road is but a sheep track and the enclosures are bounded by the horizon.'

But the fullest accounts of Club Weeks or rather Club Fortnights come from the season of 1845-6. Russell's diary records it as follows:
'Monday 17th [November]. The first day of the North Molton Meeting. [North Molton was where the kennels of the Poltimore estate were situated, but the social centre of the 'week' was the George Hotel, South Molton.] Mr Fellowes at King's Nympton Park – found in Lightly Brake, ran a ring or two but no death. N.B. Mr Fellowes gave me 'Punishment' [a hound!]. "The Ugly Buck" [his mount].
Tuesday 18th. Mr Trelawney at Heasley Mills. Found in Long Wood,

ran two or three rings round Shorticombe, Battery etc and killed in one hour at North Radworthy. "The Ghost". "Serva" having been seized with inflammation on his kidneys on the way to cover.

Wednesday 19th. The North Devon Hounds at Kensford Water, but the weather being too bad for the Moor, drew Beetleigh Wood – blank – found in Liddycombe Brake, just above Filedon, going away to Yard Down, Sherracombe and across the valley, when this gallant varmint broke the Moor Wall and faced the open with 20 couple on his brush! He then turned to the left and made his point to Cadeworthy nearly good, but the hounds pressed him so sharply against the wind that he was obliged to change his course when he boldly faced the hill, and leaving Sittabarrow on his left went away over Lord Morley's allotment to Cornham Ford and over the hill under Cornham to Simonsbath, going I believe immediately before the windows of the house, up the Exford road, when he turned to the right into the Plantation, breaking from thence into the great field by Windsticken House, going down the valley to Flexbarrow, Cow Castle and Ferny Ball, and up the banks of the Willingford Water for half a mile, when he turned up over Sheardowon Cleave and gained its summit, but here his strength failed him, he stopped in a rush bush and allowed the hounds to get up to him and was killed in the meadow under Ferny Ball House. Computed distance by Mr Knight [a Simonsbath man] 18 miles. Mr Tilbury's "Comedy". Time one hour and twenty minutes.

Thursday 20th. Sir Walter Carew at White Post, Molland Common. Found in West Molland Wood and killed a very bad, short running fox in less than an hour under Pulsworthy House. "The Bison".

Friday 21st. Mr Trelawny on Yard Down. Found in the little brake opposite Sherracombe Wood, a single hound viewing him across the field and the pack breaking the fence, almost with him. He turned it to the left and cross'd the valley, going over Whitefield Down almost to Cadeworthy, when he turned up over the Common, leaving Sittabarrow to the left and put his head straight for Simonsbath, the hounds all but flying. Here it was said they changed foxes, but however that might be, they kept their line, with no diminution of scent thro' the Plantations to Cloven Rock, down over the Warren and up the opposite side, which they kept for more than a mile and then recross'd the valley just behind the Gallon House, pointing for Exford, when he again cross'd the valley and was lost near Alderman's Barrow. This was a most beautiful run indeed. "Comedy". Mrs Horndon, Mrs Earle and Mrs Russell went well the whole of the run. The latter rode over the boundary wall at the back of the Gallon House, I measured it: a drop of 7 feet and about 5 feet high on the moor side.

Saturday 22nd. The NDH at Bray Ford. Found in twenty minutes in Gratton Wood, had a beautiful run of one hour and forty minutes over

Sholesborough Castle, Goat Hill, Chapman Barrows, crossing Swincombe Cleaves and keeping outside the Moor wall on Challacombe Common to nearly Broken Barrow Two gates, when he turn'd to the left, going down over Whitefield Enclosures to Sharland and across Bratton Down to Leworthy Village, just above which place the hounds were with difficulty stopp'd at 5 o' clock. Mr Houlditch's grey "The Owl". N.B. At three o' clock on this eventful morning the hounds broke into the feeding yard and fill'd themselves with the food prepared for their evening's meal, which accounts for the lateness of the find.

Monday 24th. Mr Trelawney at North Molton Village. Drew the Park, South Radworthy and Barkham, again blank. Found in Long Wood, ran a ring round Bettleigh, Buttery Long Stone Wells and lost under South Radworthy Wood. Found a second in Oldridge Wood, ran to Whitcot and changed and gave it up. "Serva".

Tuesday 25th. The NDH at Kensford Water on Exmoor. Drew Ricksy Ball, Little Combe and Birch Cleave; blank. Came on a drag in Orson Combe and whilst I was off my horse trying the earth, a fox was tally'd behind us and the hounds were laid on heel, they went back nearly opposite Simonsbath, then turn'd and brought the scent back to Deer Park Lodge, a few hundred yards only from the spot on which the party were standing whilst I was at the earth . Here I met them, cantered with them down to the riverside opposite Flexbarrow, where they hit the scent, going away at a very merry pace to Cow Castle, Lanacre Brake, across the Exford Road and over the river a little above the bridge, up over Withypool Common, where the hunting of the hounds was much admired, and thence to Well and across the river Barle to Bradley, Westwater and North Barton Wood near Dulverton, where they killed him. Time one hour and thirty five minutes. "Comedy".

Wednesday 26th. Sir Walter Carew at Head Gate near Twitchen. Found in White Chapel Eastern Wood, but the weather was so very wet and boisterous that we could do nothing. "The Owl".

Thursday 27th. The NDH at Bish Mill. Drew Blastridge and Hague Plantation, blank. Found in Hill Town Brake, he broke immediately and went away over the hill nearly to Meshaw Parsonage and back again to Yard, pace very good, from thence down to Rodsworthy and up the bottom to Kidland Wood, where the whole pack changed on a fresh fox, rattling him back most merrily to Week Wood, where they view'd him, and, as none of the field then knew that we had changed foxes, of course we expected to kill him every moment, but he soon undeceived us by boldly facing the hill as tho' he intended to try our mettle over Ash Moor, but before he reached it he turn'd to the right and again sunk the valley, which he kept to Hill Town Moor, the hounds running for him all the way. He then crossed the brook, and after a circle round Slew,

Waterhouse, he was view'd to ground in the brake immediately above Bish Mill. Time two hours and five minutes. "Blackberry". The hounds did their work most satisfactorily. Mrs Russell and Mrs Horndon were at the meet, but the latter only rode the chase – and did it most gallantly and altho' it was then half past five o' clock, as soon as the "whowhoop" was sounded, she trotted off to Tordown, a distance of 10 miles, dined and was at the Ball Room at South Molton at nine!!!!'

In February 1846 occurred the second meeting of the 'Exmoor Forest Hunt Club'. As before, Newton Fellowes' pack provided the sport on the first Monday and the last Saturday, Russell's and Trelawny's hunted two days each week and one day each week was provided by the Tiverton Hounds. One of Russell's North Devon Hunt days was spectacular. 'Found in Gratton wood, going away over Lydcot to Cadeworthy, Whitefield Down and up the Combe to Sittabarrow, down over Acland's allotment to Cornham and up the hill to Easthead where he broke the Moor wall out on Cheriton Ridge, when the hounds laid themselves out and, with "heads up and sterns down", raced him over Cheriton Ridge, Furze Hill and Lynn Commons, expecting every moment to catch him, but unfortunately he had just strength enough to gain the Rock near the Summer House in Lynn Cleave, where we were obliged to leave him. "Blackberry". N.B. This run was pronounced by Harry Terrell, no bad judge, to be the "best he ever saw". The distance was full 18 miles, time one hour and twenty minutes. Seven or eight horsemen out of 140 who appeared at the coverside saw the race of the last 7 miles over the Commons, where it was acknowledged by all that "Blackberry" had the best of it. The Fox [or Vicky] was caught the following Monday night in a hatch trap by Mr Yelland, whom I kept there for the purpose, brought back here and liberated the next evening.'

Another point about this second meeting of the Exmoor Forest Hunt Club is that Russell pointedly did not attend either of the two meetings held by the Tiverton Hounds. To have missed one might be put done to an indisposition or, unlikely, a prior engagement; to have missed both must have been deliberate. Which brings us to Sir Walter Palk Carew of Haccombe, whom Russell had known since the early 1820s when Sir Walter had had a stall in Charles Harris' St Hubert's Hall, and was a neighbour of the Templers of Stover. The motto above Sir Walter's stall was 'Animo non Astutia', which means, 'With spirit but not wisdom', aptly referring not only to his character but also to his drinking. Sir Walter married Ann Taylor, one of the extremely beautiful daughters of General Taylor, a Teign Valley neighbour of the Palk Carews. Ann's sisters married William Fortescue and Lord Willoughby de Broke, her father was a friend of both the Duke of Wellington and of William IV and her brother became an equerry of his widowed Queen, Adelaide. Sir Walter himself was extremely wealthy, not only being sole inheritor of his father's Carew estates, but also of the large Palk estates and was very well connected. He was a 'character', with the physique and resources to be so on a gargantuan scale. Most of the Carew ladies seem to have kept diaries, details of which have been used as the basis of a most entertaining book *Combat and Carnival* by Peter Carew and it is clear that Sir Walter and Russell were friends and that Russell was also liked by the Reverend Fitzwilliam Taylor, Sir Walter's brother-in -law who gloried in the unusual title Archpriest of Haccombe. This Haccombe living was in the gift of Sir Walter and its title a quaint pre-Reformation survival, whose importance in the nineteenth century was that the Archpriest was an Archiepiscopal peculiar, i.e. out of the authority of the Bishop of Exeter, our old friend Phillpotts.

Russell's friendship with Sir Walter probably developed after the move to Swimbridge, which brought Russell into closer contact with the Fortescues at Filleigh. It seems that Russell made up a party with Carew and William Fortescue to visit London for Queen Victoria's coronation in June 1838. During the visit Sir Walter attended one of the receptions given by Dr Howley, the Archbishop of Canterbury who, after dinner, invited questions about Church matters. Sir Walter jumped in and demanded that Howley tell the Bishop of Exeter, who was also present, 'to keep his Rural Deans in order and to forbid them to trespass on his preserves. He informed the Archbishop that on several occasions he had had to see them off the premises.'

During this London visit the party attended Ascot. Lady Carew's diary for June 16th, 1838: 'A great concourse of people to-day. The Queen...was only received tolerably well...and few of the gentlemen took off their hats... All the world went to the Royal Stand. There we met Lord Palmerston [then Liberal M.P. for Tiverton and so known to the Fortescues] who introduced us to Lord Melbourne, who seemed never to leave the Queen's side. We were presented quite informally to the Queen by Lord Melbourne, and she remembered Harriet and myself from Mr Hayter's portrait. The gentlemen would not come on to the Royal Stand, but went instead to the Jockey Club where they found a common sort of man to make bets with. I was very surprised at Mr Russell doing this as he is a clergyman.'

The sisters, Ann Carew and Harriet Fortescue were intimate with Ann Burdett-Coutts and through her they obtained an invitation to join the Duke of Wellington's party to a ball at the Palace. Their husbands decided to go to Greenwich by steamer and have a whitebait supper on their own [with Russell?]. At the ball Lady Carew danced with Louis Napoleon and Harriet 'was introduced to a funny Jewish looking man, a Mr Disraeli, who is Member for Maidstone.' The next day General Taylor came up from Devon to join the Duke and was furious to learn of the way his daughters had been treated by his sons-in-law and doubly so when he called at their hotel to find that they had gone to see a cockfight. Whether Russell joined them in the cock-pit cannot be proved or disproved.

A pleasant vignette of this friendship is recorded by the Carew ladies as follows. Returning from a shopping expedition to Torquay on a Saturday, they were surprised to hear singing emanating from the parish church which was next to Haccombe House. On investigating, Lady Ann and her sister found the choir being rehearsed in *From Greenland's icy mountains* by Sir Walter and Jack Russell, both in full hunting gear. At their approach the singing stopped and Sir Walter bellowed: 'Just come in from hunting. Jack's staying the night and will take the service to-morrow.' During the service the organ, played by Lady Carew and reliant on being pumped by hand, performed erratically and Russell took as his text 'For this relief much thanks' and preached an excellent extempore sermon.

During the 1830s and 1840s Sir Walter was mad keen on hunting and shooting. On a trip to France, which inevitably began with a bust up in the Customs' shed when a damned foreigner wanted to inspect his luggage, Sir Walter, sitting on the top of the coach, his invariable custom as he hated closed windows, took pot shots at birds as they progressed southwards, on one occasion narrowly missing a gendarme. The Carew diaries throw extra light on a South Molton Week. Sir Walter stayed at the George Hotel with the lads, while his wife was invited to stay with the Fortescues at Filleigh. On the 26th November 1845 [in *Combat and Carnival* the day is given as the 16th, which was a Sunday and therefore an error] that day when the weather was so 'boisterous' the Filleigh Ladies came to the meet in two closed barouches and the following dialogue took place as Sir Walter approached the cabs and addressed his wife. 'You had as well stayed at home. What's the use of coming hunting in a cab?' From the other cab Lady Fortescue asked 'Sir Walter pray tell me where we can best see the hounds cast off.' Sir Walter refused to answer beyond making an unfavourable comparison between her and Penelope Russell who was on horseback. Lady Fortescue responded 'I have two carriages of young ladies and must devote my time to them'. 'Don't you believe it Maam. Time is wasted on women which you can give to hounds,' was the polite riposte.

From other sources Peter Carew constructed the following account of a dinner of the Club in the George Hotel. 'It was a lively party with six Masters of Foxhounds present. Mr Trelawny was in the chair and he records that Sir John Rogers and Admiral Rogers, his brother, both hard hunting South Devon sportsmen, kept the ball rolling with unceasing gaiety. "We drank to fox-hunting several times over. I sat next to Sir Walter Carew who stuck to his port like a man flooring his two bottles in orthodox style, the rest drank punch. After dinner there was a sale of horses by auction". This was a custom from Chulmleigh Club days when the owner was allowed one bid and one bid only when his horse was put up. On this occasion the port had got to Sir Walter and he bought a large number of horses at an exorbitant price and had a row with his cousin Tom Carew, who took objection to Sir Walter calling Bishop Phillpotts "a miserable old crow" and threw the butter dish at Sir Walter. Only with difficulty did the rest of the company prevent the Carews from coming to blows.'

Later that season the Carew diaries report on another visit of the Sir Walter and Lady Anne to Filleigh where the Duke of Wellington and Lord Palmerston were house guests. Palmerston's eye for a pretty woman was probably the key to the invitation. At a dinner during the visit the Russells were invited and Jack Russell was invited to say grace and 'the reverend gentleman's mind was presumably elsewhere for he started "For what we are about to receive the Lord give us good hunting". After the ladies had retired Palmerston found Sir Walter heavy going . The next day a hunt was organised to amuse the Duke and Sir Walter disgraced himself by over indulgence of stirrup-cups, knocked over a servant carrying a tray of bottles and after an unskilful hour called the day off. If these events took place they must have been before December 13th when Russell became ill and housebound for almost a month. They probably did happen as they explain why Sir Walter largely gave up hunting in Devon in 1846 and gave up his pack before the second meeting of the Club. What hunting he then did seems to have been in Leicestershire and anyway he had discovered a new interest: yachting, in which he also involved Russell. In the early 1840s something or someone gave Sir Walter the idea of building himself a yacht. Never one to do things by halves he got Sir William Symonds, the designer of the Royal Yacht, the *Victoria and Albert*, to design an hundred ton sailing yacht, 'None of your infernal engines in her, mind. I want fresh air and not to be smoked by steam and soot; it may do for the Queen and that German feller, but not for me.' His yacht, the *Beatrice* was built at Torquay and she was launched in April 1845. Taylor connections procured the services of Queen Adelaide for the occasion. Lord Palmerston was also there, perhaps more interested in the charms of

Lady Ann than in those of Sir Walter, and so was the First Lord of the Admiralty. Dinner at the Imperial Hotel followed during which Sir Walter punctuated the toast to 'Her Majesty's Ministers' with 'and damnation to the Income Tax'. In August 1845 the *Beatrice* was fitted out and ready for a trial run. Sir Walter, William Fortescue, Lord Willoughby de Broke, the Rev. Fitzwilliam Taylor and the Rev. John Russell made up the party. Sir Walter had hired a new cook for the occasion, a Mrs Hext, who had to replace Mrs Haigh, a Scots lady of spirit equal to Sir Walter's, who, in a memorable parting interview with her employer, retorted 'Let me tell ye, sir, that you're six feet three of the verra worse stuff wrapped up in one bundle.'

Fitzwilliam Taylor recorded the voyage in his journal. '25th August. Got under way about noon. Fine day not much wind, had a tiring trip up to Cowes; found a rolling swell outside when Jack Russell was very seasick and could not eat any dinner which was as well as the cook, Mrs Hext, was so ill herself that none was prepared. Walter was so angry that he said he would get rid of her in Alderney.

26th August. Fine day and beautiful breeze. The cook got better and cooked such a beautiful dinner that Walter forgot his annoyance of yesterday.'

However Russell was persuaded to renew his acquaintance with the *Beatrice* on other occasions, but probably did not go to sea in her again. One such was a Plymouth Regatta when *Beatrice* won the Royal Western Yacht Club Cup and Lord Mount Edgcumbe gave a party. Sir Walter's youngest daughter Bessie recorded the occasion: 'We all enjoyed ourselves at Mount Edgcumbe, where we met all sorts of notabilities. Lord and Lady Fortescue and Mr Hugh Fortescue who are relations of Uncle Forty [William Fortescue], who says he is the ignoble branch of the family. There was a funny old clergyman, Mr Russell, who keeps a pack of hounds and breeds terriers; they call him the "Sporting Parson". He and Uncle Fitz [the Archpriest of Haccombe, Fitzwilliam Taylor] are great friends, having the same tastes. The Bishop of Exeter, Dr Phillpotts, was also there; Uncle Fitz does not get on very well with him; I think because the Bishop tries to keep him in order, but does not succeed. A very happy day.'

If little girls in South Devon knew Russell was called 'the Sporting Parson' then those who knew about hunting were loud in his praise. As the years rolled by and he moved from his fifties to his sixties the tributes poured in, especially after he had to give up the Mastership of the North Devon Hunt so that he became virtually MFH emeritus for the whole of fox-hunting-land. In October 1859 he was guest of honour at a grand occasion at Eggesford House where he was presented with what the press described as a 'superb epargne', inscribed: 'Presented to the Reverend John Russell by upwards of a hundred of his friends as a mark of their respect and esteem'. Lord Portsmouth was deputed by the donors to make the presentation and he stated that the presentation was not only to mark his fame as a sportsman who had led the North Devon Hounds for so long, but also it was to show how heartily they valued the character he had maintained throughout life. 'Few men have so many friends as Jack Russell, who meets a welcome in every home he visits. It arose from the kindness of his heart and the warmth of his character'. Rather pertinently his Lordship continued by saying that he had never heard that he had ever in a single instance neglected his duties as a clergyman. In his reply Russell mentioned his having given up the Mastership of NDH, that he had advertised the Pack and that a 'lord' had offered to become the new Master if Russell could get £600 a year in subscriptions. Russell said he had replied; 'If I could only get £300 a year I would not be troubling you!' Russell also referred to his long friendship with the Portsmouths which dated from his first meeting with Newton Fellowes in 1810 when he had stayed at the 'old house by the church'. He ended his speech of thanks very elegantly with the words 'I thank you all most heartily, but I can never offer you thanks enough for your kindness, and I will conclude by addressing you individually in the words of our immortal bard. May you

"Live longer than I have time to tell your years;
And when old Time shall lead you to the tomb,
May goodness and you fill up one monument."

'The party then adjourned to the field', continued the *North Devon Journal*, 'where 200 horsemen joined in the chase... The party then returned, wet and weary, to again partake of the hospitality of the mansion. We hear of but one instance in which the liberality of the noble lord was abused. A man with a moustache, who claimed to represent the 'cheap' press indulged himself in potent liquors until he became thoroughly intoxicated and so offensive he was expelled from the house. Late in the afternoon we saw him led down to Eggesford station with a railway ticket stuck to his back "For Barnstaple – per Goods Train – not returnable – to be kept DRY".'

In 1860 Russell was invited to a presentation to Lord Poltimore of a large canvas of the Poltimore Hunt executed by Widgery. The occasion was a large dinner at the Poltimore Arms and Russell's task was to propose the toast of the young Lord Poltimore's infant son Coplestone Bampfylde. The press records him doing so wittily and elegantly in a speech which emphasised his long connections with the family. He said 'the subject of the toast was a very beautiful one, but he feared he could hardly do it justice, although he ought to be able to do so, inasmuch as he had always, for the last twenty years, whenever there had been a meeting, either of a private or public character, had the honour of giving the health of the father, the present Lord Poltimore. Although too young to say much about at present, for his habits were not yet developed, still he could say that the heir of Poltimore was as fine a child as he had ever seen in his life. He hoped he would prove not only as fine but as good and excellent a man as his father and grandfather. In conclusion the Reverend Gentleman expressed a hope that peace and happiness might attend the young heir through all his days, and that when it might please God to remove his father he would become as good a landlord and friend as his father and grandfather had been before him.' A little butter would do no harm as his nephew Russell Riccard was bailiff and agent for the Poltimore estates in North Devon.

No Devon sporting occasion was complete without him, but his fame as the 'Sporting Parson' or as plain 'Jack Russell' became national. To mark this *Baily's Magazine* in 1865 carried a long article comparing the recently dead Squire Osbaldeston, prince of Meltonians with the still very much alive Jack Russell and in 1870 they featured him with an equally long biography to mark the occasion when he finally gave up keeping hounds for, when he gave up the Mastership of the North Devon Hunt in 1858, he kept a Cry of some ten couple and hunted on his own for pleasure, though anyone who wanted to could join him. In a letter, reproduced by *Baily's* in 1870 he described his last outing with the Cry: 'I wish you had seen my last run before Christmas, with ten couples of hounds, over Exmoor, 25 miles on the map, 18 as the crow flies, at least. Some natives say more. Not a check and only one small fence, over the best ground in the forest. We, a chosen few, were never a hundred yards from them'. Sceptics wrote into Baily's saying this was impossible, so in the first issue of 1871 witnesses revealed that 'Russell's last fox' was found in Tinnerleigh Brake, a mile east of Parracombe, it made a circuit westwards around Parracombe then made east to Friendship Inn on the northern end of Bratton Down. From Bratton Down to Stoke Pero where he was killed was 15½ miles on a direct line, but the fox did not go straight, he went via Whitefield, Withycombe, Swinscombe, across the valley to Woodbarrow and Pinkworthy Pond, over the length of The Chains to Exehead and Prayway, up the hill and over to Gallon House, now called Red Deer, then he returned to the Exe valley and to the Withypool coverts. He turned left by Exford Mill and over the Porlock road through the valley to Codsend Moor and Dunkery and down over the heath to Stoke Pero. A fitting end to his career as a huntsman with his own hounds.

By 1870 many people considered hunting an unsuitable occupation for a clergyman. Russell served Swimbridge at a time when first the High Churchmen of the Oxford Movement almost tore the Church of England apart with ritualism; then the Evangelicals tried to make it ridiculous with their gloomy excesses and unintelligent approach to scripture. In an article of August 1854 the *Sporting Magazine* took the 'Sporting Parson' issue head on. 'Devon is a sporting and hunting county. I fancy there are more sporting parsons – a good old English title, almost obsolete in these days of priests and Puseyites – in this famed county than in any four others in England. Which does not prevent their being noble hearted, Christian gentlemen and benevolent parish clergymen, doing infinitely less harm in riding to hounds than walking about dressed up like Jesuits, taking tea and talking balderdash with silly old women, outwardly declaring themselves orthodox divines and pocketing tithes, inwardly feeling as Romish priests and spending those tithes in teaching error and promoting auricular confession'. Sentiments Russell would have echoed. Once asked what he would do if given a surplice he replied that he would give it to his wife to make a night-dress. He visited when asked to come, but did not otherwise intrude. He was known and liked by his parishioners, he was a friend to the gypsies, he used his wide contacts to raise money to rebuild the parish church, the services were regularly taken, he hired a curate and he was much in demand as a preacher for charitable causes, especially the North Devon Infirmary. No doubt people heard the Christian message through him who would not otherwise have come into close contact with a clergyman. Who will cast the first stone?

Those who approach Russell via the doyen of Devon Historians, W.G. Hoskins, will have another view of Russell. Hoskins, when describing the work Canon Girdlestone of Halberton did for the agricultural labourer, referred to 'fox-hunting Squarsons, who were Christian only in the sense that they had once been baptised and, in the next sentence wrote 'the futile Parson Jack Russell'. Yet the record seems against Hoskins. Although not an agriculturalist Russell gave his countenance to the promotion of Agricultural Shows, Societies and Ploughing Matches. The *North Devon Journal* reported on the North Tawton Ploughing Match of January 1858 as something that had replaced the revels centring around drunkenness and wrestling for silver spoons in the churchyard and that at the dinner in the Three Pigeons afterwards Russell was in the chair 'whose presence was a guarantee of hilarity and good fellowship'. In February 1858 he attended a meeting of the Bath and West of England Agricultural Society at Barnstaple. In April 1858 he was elected to the Barnstaple Union Poor Law Guardians for

Swimbridge and in the same month he was the life and soul of the party at the coming of age of Augustus Bampfylde the heir to the Barony of Poltimore. In May he was present at the Great Torrington Agricultural Society Dinner. In July he attended the meeting of the Barnstaple Turnpike Trust. And these are only those 'useful' occasions that the *Journal* reported on in the first months of 1858.

Whatever one may think the life of a clergyman should be, surely the affections of his parishioners may be some clue of his worth. Some in Swimbridge and its surrounds disliked him. In the 1840s Nott of Bydown for example and in 1873 some cranks posted the following bills all over Swimbridge and Landkey: 'Matins! Villagers you are asked to attend Matins. Do you know the meaning of the term? It is not found in the Word of God, but in all Popish Books you may find it. They are wanting to teach you the way of Papacy. Look to Jesus and not to Matins or Mary. Confess not to Priests. Not Matins or Mary but the Five Wounds of Christ. Judges vi, 25-29. John iii, 16.' Though to suggest that the Anglican Church in Swimbridge as represented by Russell encouraged Catholicism was very wide of the mark and they probably chose Swimbridge for their fanatic bills because Russell's fame would get them publicity. However it is clear that Russell was extremely popular with his people as the following two episodes show. The first was the celebrations in Swimbridge to mark the marriage of the Prince of Wales to Princess Alexandra of Denmark. While his son took a prominent part in the parade of the North Devon Volunteer Forces in Barnstaple, Russell presided over the festivities in his parish. There was a dinner for 200 labourers and tradesman provided by the munificence of John Smith a wealthy parishioner, where Russell, as Chairman of the feast, proposed the health of 'The Bride and Groom' and incorporated the felicitous phrase 'it is not always that happiness went as smooth as marriage bells, but he trusted…' When the Vice Chairman proposed the health of the Chairman he said 'they all knew him. His praise was beyond the power of eloquence, so he would only give the toast: "Our Worthy Chairman". Again and again rose cheer upon cheer, till lungs were well nigh exhausted.' When he rose to reply Russell said, 'he looked upon it as a token that he was appreciated not only as a friend and neighbour but as a clergyman. He trusted that the labours of the last thirty two years had not been in vain.' The wives of these tradesmen and labourers were given a big tea. The gentry had dinner at the Lamb and Flag, followed by a ball.

Having presided at a dinner in Swimbridge Russell galloped down to Landkey, where the children had tea and cake at three o'clock, the women 'a decoctation of the fragrant leaf' at five, the working men a substantial dinner at six and the yeomen sat down to dinner with Russell as Chairman at seven. As the press put it his 'presence is always a guarantee of kind feeling and good cheer'. This is not then a picture of parishes out of tune with their incumbent.

The second occasion was ten years later. An enterprising farmer called Thomas Yeo, taking advantage of the new railway, had started up a manure business, or as we would call it a fertiliser business. In October 1873 Yeo hosted a 'Manure Audit Dinner' for forty local farmers and asked Russell to take the chair. With his usual felicity Russell thanked their host, 'He would not enter into the particulars of the merits of manures, because he saw around him the very best farmers in his own and neighbouring parishes. And if they really valued these manures they ought to feel greatly obliged to their host for introducing them and he himself was obliged to their host for the pleasure of meeting so many of his friends. They had to thank Mr Yeo for his hospitality and in pro-posing "Success to the Wellington Manure Company" he asked them to drink to the happiness of Mr and Mrs Yeo and their family'. At the end of the evening a farmer called Westcott proposed the health of the Chairman, who said that they all looked up with reverence and feelings of affection to Mr Russell as if he were a father. He had baptised nearly all of them and married a good many. The toast was received with long and continuous cheering.

Russell was not just a good fox-hunter, he was also a good parish cler-gyman, robust, life-enhancing, a man of peace and a good neighbour and friend to all classes and conditions. In a very active life he brought a natural Christianity into the hunting field, the society of the great house, the dinners, balls and galas of the middling sort, and a natural warmth of intercourse with the labouring poor. His was not a Christianity of fasting and denial, nor of sacramentalism and novel rit-ualisms, nor did he make conversation uneasy with a larding of biblical texts and a dwelling on the sinfulness of virtually everything that was fun. In his way Russell was as valuable a country clergyman as Keble, the poetry of the one and the hunting of the other both now being equally unfashionable, but both in their day ways of bringing Christianity to a larger public.

Chapter Nine

'THE SWEETEST MEMORY'

It is part of growing old that the sadnesses come, at first singly, then in battalions. In the nature of things these sadnesses came through the deaths of his friends and the misfortunes of his family. The death of his first son John Bury had made his second son Richard Bury, born in 1828 and always called 'Bury,' doubly precious. He was sent to Blundell's where his performance was mediocre. Bishop Temple's biographer described him as 'a very good natured, but lax-minded boy,' which is curious as Temple left in 1839 and Bury only arrived in 1840. But Temple maintained a fatherly interest in Blackmore, the author of *Lorna Doone*, which Blackmore resented and Blackmore was at Blundell's the whole time Bury was there, 1840-42. In 1842 a law suit between Tiverton and Blundell's concluded with the Vice Chancellor deciding that boarders could not stay at the school, so Bury went from Blundell's to Harrow from 1843-5. There is a gap then until he joined the 2nd Queen's Royal regiment of Foot in February 1848 with the rank of Ensign; he purchased a Lieutenancy in 1849 and retired by sale in June 1851, when the regiment was sent out to South Africa to take part in the Kaffir Wars. He took up a Captaincy in the North Devon Militia, then being formed as part of a defence scare, sparked off by Napoleon III's coup d'etat and the proclamation of the Second Empire. His name soon began to appear in the Barnstaple press as attending the local Military Balls and as participating in local amateur dramatics.

Although it is tempting just to write Bury off as the son of a famous father, he was obviously competent. In February 1863 he spoke a long verse prologue to an 'Amateur Dramatic Performance' for the benefit of the 6th Devon Rifle Volunteers at Barnstaple Theatre. His delivery was declared 'graceful' and 'deservedly applauded.' Being a Major, as he now had become, in the Volunteers in 1863 was to be in the forefront of local life since the country, which had been alarmed by Napoleon III's coup of December 1851, was, in the early 1860s, in the grip of a full blown invasion scare caused by the perceived aggressions of Napoleon III, who had invaded Austrian Italy in 1859 and in 1863 had set up a puppet French Empire in Mexico. The last of Bury's Prologue ran

'Who knows against whom he next may draw the sword?
What then to do? this rage how to control
And check the visions of that troubled soul?
England well knew, and starting at her word,
A hundred thousand men seized on the sword,
Pledg'd all our soil inviolate to maintain
From every foe, and thrust him out again;
'Defence, and not Defiance' all their end,
Fearing no foe and greeting every friend…

No foreign foe shall dare this land assail,
Conscious that here he never shall prevail.
To this support that at your hands we ask,
This well filled house shows that you support the task,
'Tis thus by coming here your presence cheers
And proves you like your Local Volunteers.

Another press account refers to 'both the Major and his Corps being public favourites.' Certainly, Bury was a regular attender at banquets in North Devon and equally regularly he was the respondent to the toasts to 'The Armed Services and the Volunteers Forces.' In fact 1863 was a busy year for the Volunteers and Bury took as important a part in the parade of the Volunteers in honour of the Prince of Wales wedding as his father in the less martial celebrations in Swimbridge. In a dinner during May in the Barnstaple Assembly Rooms, given for the Sixth Devon Rifle Volunteers and the Yeomanry, he sounded off with a par- ticularly fiery speech – 'I beg to thank you heartily for the compliment you have paid to the Sixth Devon Rifle Volunteers, whom I have the honour to command, in drinking their health. I believe the corps is only too happy to see our brother corps, the Yeomanry, in Barnstaple. As regards any rivalry that exists among us – the only rivalry between us is – "Who will be the first to drive away the invader?"' Later in the week's joint training he took part in a football match between the Sixth Devon Volunteers led by himself and the Yeomanry led by Lt Colonel Sir Arthur Chichester and Cornet the Honourable Mark Rolle. In the winter of 1862-3 he also hunted. Bury was in the mainstream of Barnstaple life in the early 1860s.

For full-time work he went into the bank with which his grandfather, the Admiral, had had connections and in 1866 married Mary Ann, the daughter of Gilbert Knill Cotton a prosperous merchant of Barnstaple. In 1866 trade directories list Bury as living in South Molton at 64, South Street, managing the South Molton branch of the West of England and South Wales Bank and being a Borough Magistrate and J.P. In 1876, when his mother's relative Henry Dene retired, he became the manager of the Barnstaple Branch and took over Dennington House at Swimbridge after his mother's death in 1875, when his father returned to Tordown, with a housekeeper, Mary Cockings, to look after him. Bury also had a house at Trafalgar Lawn, Barnstaple, and rose to be Lt Colonel in the Militia. It seemed that son Bury had established himself, but sadly the Bank collapsed in 1878 and Bury, by then a Director, was involved in the bankruptcy proceedings. For many years the Bank had paid generous, perhaps overgenerous dividends and many widows and spinsters were reliant on it for their whole incomes. Its collapse was a very serious regional event, caused largely by the world depression which began in the mid 1870s and by incautious loans made by the South Wales branches. Bury became ill about 1878 and died a few months after his father in 1883.

Russell's wife Penelope sickened sometime around 1870 and died in 1875. She had always been a shadowy figure and it is difficult to gauge whether Russell was saddened or relieved at her passing. Otter Davies quotes a letter from Russell about her final illness – 'The dear old missis is, I grieve to say, very ill; and I can't leave her for many hours together. Still she is cheerful when anyone comes in, and WILL, as usual, stir her stumps to make them comfortable. But that sort of exertion does her no good; and sometimes I am led to believe she can't live through the day.' Her death, on January 1st 1875, increased his financial problems. By the end of the 1870s his own family's prospects compared unfavourably with the Bencrafts, his in-laws on his wife's side, and the Riccards his other in-laws. His brother-in-law Stephen Bencraft continued to be a force in Barnstaple politics, a successful lawyer and a man of enterprise who patented Bencraft's Saddle in the early 1840s. One of his sons Lionel who died in 1892 was for forty years Town Clerk of Barnstaple. His other in-laws, the Riccards, dominated South Molton. His other brother-in-law James Riccard was also a successful lawyer and often Mayor, his son Russell Martyn Riccard was Town Clerk of South Molton from 1861-79, and his grandson Russell Louis Riccard also became Town Clerk. Another nephew of Russell's became a doctor and was the first in the area to use an anaesthetic. The Riccards were also the agents for managing the extensive Poltimore properties. Both the Bencrafts and the Riccards were solid and successful.

Eventually Russell must have become as virtually bankrupt as his son Bury was to be after 1879. Luckily his friends came to the rescue. In 1879 Lord Poltimore appointed him to the Rectory of Black Torrington, with a stipend twice that of Swimbridge, and his wealthy friends had a whip round, presumably to clear off the more pressing debts. On July 2nd, 1880 there was a grand presentation at the Duke of Bedford's house at Eaton Square where Russell was presented with a silver soup tureen, a purse of 650 gold sovereigns and an illuminated book containing the names of the 158 subscribers. These names are a ringing testimony to Russell's fame and popularity. The list is headed by the Prince of Wales, the Bishop of Exeter, a Duke [Bedford], three Earls, [Fortescue, Portsmouth and Rocksavage], Lords Beresford, Wolverton and Ebrington, the Countess of Lovelace, Lady Westbury, the Hon. Mark Rolle, no less than eight MFHs and a roll call of Devon names: Bulteel, Carew, Daniel, Karslake, Trefusis and Trelawny. Earl Fortescue made the presentation, paying 'high tribute to Mr Russell as a man, a sportsman and a clergyman. His Lordship also paid a high tribute to the reverend gentleman for his kindly work in his late parish and for his charity and Christian love, which augured well for his success amongst his new parishioners.' And Russell replied as follows 'in a voice that showed how painfully he was affected by allusions to the past: "My Lords, Ladies and Gentlemen, I must plead for your kind indulgence today. My heart is full and you will, I hope, pardon its overflowing. When, but a short time hence, it became known to me that a testimonial was in contemplation for me, I felt that I had no claims for such a recognition - that it was the outcome of the kindness of my friends, and there was no sufficient merit of my own to lead them thus to rally round me. I hear that to my good friends at Taunton, Dr and Mrs Kingslake, I am in great degree indebted for the origination of the idea which has brought such honour to me. Trusty and true for many a long year have they been to me, and I gladly acknowledge my debt of gratitude to them; but the generous and prompt response which has been made on all sides to the proposal well nigh overwhelms me. His Royal Highness the Prince of Wales, with that kindness and generosity which are so characteristic of him, has done me the great honour of heading the list, thus adding one more to the many favours he has already conferred on me. No less can I value the countenance of my good, kind and considerate Bishop. Then I must advert specially to one who for many years has aided me so generously for many years in all works for the good of my late parish, the Duke of Bedford, who has so kindly and considerately given us his residence to-day. To Lord Fortescue I owe so much as one of the best of friends and kindest of neighbours; and to his eldest son, Lord Ebrington, I know I am deeply indebted for his unwearied exertions in connection with this testimonial. I must not omit to mention the many obligations I am under to each and all of the family at Eggesford; and further I wish to express my gratitude to my good friend and patron, Lord Poltimore, to whom I am indebted for my present preferment. Ladies and Gentlemen, I should like to refer by name to many others who have been most generous and who have oft and oft done for me many a kind act, but I know that to-day I must address you collectively. From the bottom of my heart then, let me tender you my most sincere thanks for this magnificent gift with which you have presented me. I am now, as you well know, an old man of more than four score years, and I could not have anticipated that my declining years could have been marked by so bright a pleasure as that with which you have showered upon me. I must thank his Lordship for the very kind manner in which he referred to my parochial duties at Swimbridge. I can only say that it has always been my earnest endeavour to do my duty to those, to whom , I trust, I have been not less a pastor than a friend. I may here advert to the many kind testimonial presents I have also received from my neighbours, including some of the very poorest of my parishioners. I shall bear away with me from this place one of the happiest memories of my long life, and, if at any time hereafter I should chance to be hipped or depressed, as I am feign to confess I have been of late, I will conjure up to mind the remembrance of to-day as a bright recollection to scatter away every sorrow. Once again thanking all those who are now present, as well as those of my good friends who are absent, I will say to each and all "God bless you".'

The Prince of Wales he had met for the first time in August 1865 at Plymouth when the Prince and Princess came to grace the meeting of the Royal Agricultural Show held there. Although the press did not mention Russell's attendance at the public functions, Otter Davies asserted that the attendance of Russell at a private dinner was procured through Lord Beresford, who was Flag Officer to the Admiral in charge of the Dockyard and who had met Russell because he hunted with Trelawney's Hounds. The Russell charm must have had its effect because the Prince remembered him. In 1873 Russell visited Henry Villebois of Marham in Norfolk, to whom he had sold his last hounds, a neighbour to the Prince at Sandringham. Villebois' party were invited to a Ball on a Friday night at Sandringham, where Russell danced till 4.00 a.m., then got the train back to Swimbridge to do duty on the Sunday. Not bad for rising seventy-seven years old. He was invited again to Sandringham after Christmas. The local press announced the visit thus, 'The friends of the Reverend Jack Russell, and few men have more friends, will be gratified at hearing that… the reverend gentleman was present at the recent ball held at Sandringham. They will be still more pleased that the Princess did Mr Russell the further honour of bespeaking his presence at Sandringham on a visit in the early days of next year, when she hoped to have the pleasure of listening to a sermon from him at the parish church on the Sunday. We do not know if our popular sporting parson has ever had the honour of preaching before royalty, but those who know his ability and the clear and pleasant voice which almost eighty years have left him unimpaired, will have no doubt that he will acquit himself as much to the satisfaction of his royal listeners in his clerical capacity as his graceful and genial manners make him the most welcome of guests in society and his accomplishments as a sportsman leave him no rival in the field'.

Before going to Sandringham he spent Christmas week as the house guest of the Fortescues at Castle Hill. His second visit to Sandringham was fully described by Russell to his friend and memorialist, Otter Davies, and three incidents stand out. At dinner the first day the Prince noticed Russell sending off for a second helping of fish and later gave the servants orders always to offer him 'seconds' of the fish course. The first evening's dinner ended with a bottle of 1820 Port, which Russell appreciated. On the second night a different port was offered, the Prince asked him how he liked it and Russell replied 'very good sir, but not quite as stout a wine as the port you gave me last night'. In future, whatever the rest of the company had, a bottle of '20 port was before Russell. He endured one of the Prince's practical jokes, which everyone found so funny. One of the other members of the party was a Mr Hammond, whose hounds were to meet the following day nearby and a telegram was brought to that gentleman, who, as prearranged, passed it to the Prince to read. It ran 'From Bill George, Canine Castle, Kensal Green to Anthony Hammond Esq., Sandringham, Wolverton. The Rev. John Russell having disappointed me in not calling for a bagman as he passed through London, shall send him by first train to Wolverton. Hope he will arrive fresh.' Mirth and amusement unconfined.

At the Sandringham tenants' ball Princess Alexandra specially asked to dance with Russell and they saw the new year in on the dance floor. He also spent some time of his ten day visit alone with the Princess and her two boys, then aged nine and eight, the older being already a cause of anxiety to his parents for his slowness. At the end of the visit he shared the Prince's coach as far as London.

Russell's relationship with the Waleses continued to deepen. When Penelope Russell died they sent him a letter of condolence and in 1876 he was again their guest at Sandringham. In July 1878 the Waleses came to the Passing Out Parade at H.M.S. *Britannia* at Dartmouth. A special train was laid on to Kingsbridge, where a special station was constructed opposite *Britannia* and red carpet laid from the carriage door to the water. A cutter coxed by their eldest son Prince Edward, the Duke of Clarence, with Prince George as one of the crew conveyed Their Royal Highnesses to *Britannia*, where among those present was Russell. After the ceremonies the party returned to the station and the Princess took into her coach the two Princes, Lady Beresford, Miss Knollys, the boys' private tutor, the Reverend J.M. Dalton and the Reverend John Russell. Presumably Russell left the party at Taunton or Exeter to return to Swimbridge, but he was obviously an intimate.

When the Prince came west on a stag hunting visit and stayed at Dunster Castle in August 1879, it was natural for Russell to be one of the house party. An excess of royalism affected the West Country. Crowds thronged all the stations from Taunton to Dunster to cheer the Royal Party, which consisted of Prince Louis of Battenburg, Lord Charles Beresford, Admiral of the Fleet Sir Henry Keppel and a sprinkling of equerries. The house party at Dunster Castle included Mrs Bosanquet, Mrs Granville Somerset and, of course, Jack Russell. The meet next day was at Hawkcombe Head and the Prince travelled there in a carriage with his host, Mr Luttrell, Prince Louis and Russell. It is said that a farmer, seeing Russell in a carriage rather than on horseback, remarked that it happened to all of us eventually, 'You can't have two forenoons in one day'. At Hawkcombe the Royal party saw a crowd of up to 10,000, of whom perhaps 2000 were mounted. 'His Royal Highness drove round the field and was received with every demonstration of loyalty. Subsequently he and his party partook of luncheon'. [*North Devon Journal*.] The afternoon's hunt was rather cluttered, but eventually a stag was brought to bay in Badgworthy Water and killed thus – 'The huntsman handed the knife to the Prince, who gave the coup de grace to the royal quarry and was immediately "blooded" by Mr Joyce'. [*North Devon Journal*.] The party then returned by carriage to Dunster.

Earlier in the year Russell had gone north to stay with one of the nineteenth century's greatest hunting men, John [Jack] Anstruther Thomson of Charleton, Fife. Jack Thomson wrote his memoirs and used some letters Russell had written him, which reveal something of the vigour of the old man, who was eighty-three, and of the state of Bury's health. 'Tordown 13th March. I am just starting for Trafalgar Lawn and will report progress before I close this letter. I have so made up my mind to start on Monday morning for the Land o' Cakes that I shall not only be grieved on Bury's account, but sadly disappointed on my own, if I cannot do so. As you do not hunt till Wednesday, I shall take it quietly and sleep in London; if I do make a start of it on Monday night, a young widow, whom I am engaged to marry – not to myself, but to another –

will, I know, take me in and do for me. She is a sister of Froude Bellew's wife, and a big 'un for a youngster! All kind regards, etc.

P.S. Trafalgar Lawn 5.45 Bury is mending, though not well enough to leave his bed, but he wishes me to go to you on Monday, and so I shall start accordingly, at least I hope so.' During his visit to Charleton he went to a ball, dined out most nights and hunted twice.

In the days after his return he wrote two further letters to Thomson. 'Tordown, Monday Morning, 31st March, 1879. I arrived safely at South Molton station on Saturday and yesterday went through my usual duties in Swimbridge church. Another letter arrived from Lady Portsmouth begging me to dine and sleep at Eggesford today to meet Lord Camperdown, whoever he may be, so I am off again! and tomorrow go to Ivybridge [for a hunt followed by a dinner]. I can't find words strong enough to express my thanks to yourself and Mrs Thomson, including "Rosie" [their daughter] for all your kindness to me; but I am very grateful, as I ought to be, for it, and wish I could return it in kind at once. But a few more months and we shall be in the heart of the stag-hunting season, when you have promised to bring them both to my little Alpine cottage [as he called Tordown], and when Mary and I will try to take care of you all. She, the said Mary, desires me to return you the very best thanks for your most liberal, kind and handsome present, which, she says will last her all her life. I will give you some account of the sport at Ivybridge as soon as I can. With best and kindest love to you all, I am, my dear Jack, ever yours affectionately J. Russell.'

Further letters went to Charleton in April and June. In April he sent two terriers by hamper to Thomson and asked that some potatoes be sent back in it. In June he wrote from Colliepriest House, Tiverton where he was staying to attend an Old Blundellian meeting, and mentioned that he was due in London in July to marry Lord Rocksavage. In July he had to write to Thomson to warn that he had to be involved in the Prince of Wales' visit, which would clash with Thomson's visit to Tordown. 'Tordown, 28th July. PRIVATE. The Prince of Wales comes to Dunster Castle on Thursday the 21st of August to hunt with the stag hounds near Porlock on the 22nd and will be off to Devonport on the 23rd and Colonel Kingscote [the Prince's equerry] writes to say, and so does Mrs Luttrell, that I am to meet him there. That circumstance, however, need make no difference to you or yours, for Mary will take care of you for the few hours I shall be absent. The Prince says he will not come at all if his advent is advertised in the papers... The stag hound fixtures are: Tuesday 12th August Cloutsham; Friday 15th Hawkcombe Head. I want to keep the latter for the 22nd, but the first four days are always in the Porlock country. My horses will meet you anywhere and on any day you name.' Further letters report that in early August he drove himself and Mary the 60 miles round trip to Black Torrington to inspect the Rectory and that he stag hunted on the 12th, getting home after a full day in the saddle after ten o'clock, and again on the 15th and 18th. Thomson describes the end of the 'Prince's' Hunt on the 22nd. 'Several stags were soon on foot and one was sailing away towards Badsworthy Wood. I don't know where they ran to, but it was a sort of semicircle, and luckily the Prince nicked in and saw the finish in the river near the Doones' houses. The stag turned upstream with the hounds in view; they drove him up and down the stream and pulled him down. Arthur got hold and gave his knife to the Prince, who gave the coup de grace. There was a crowd in the path in front of me, and I scrambled down a steep place to where the Prince was standing. He had a patch of blood on his cheek, one of the farmers having taken the liberty of 'blooding' him.'

A final visit to Sandringham took place in 1882, on which occasion the Prince and Princess gave him a horseshoe diamond pin. Otter Davies quoted the following conversation. When pinning the horseshoe into Russell's scarf, the Prince said 'There now, it looks quite clerical'. 'But,' said Russell, bowing to the royal pair, 'may I ask if it is given conjointly?' 'Yes, of course, conjointly,' replied the Princess with a charming smile.' I suspect that there was a tendresse between the old widowed clergyman and the increasingly lonely Princess of Wales, who was treating her husband's continuous infidelities with admirable, but probably painful, dignity.

In an age when the earlier public mood of anti-royalism was swinging towards the royalty worship of the Jubilees, Russell's friendship with the Waleses, together with his own standing as the 'Sporting Parson' ensured a busy life for his old age. His family's connection with Blundell's and his own fondness for the school led to his going back again and again to Old Boys Days in the 1870s and early 1880s when the school was refounding itself and moving to a new site. Perhaps the new headmaster, A.L. Francis, rather milked the popularity of the old man, but it is a testimony to his fame that the School Steeplechase, initiated in the 1870s, was renamed 'The Russell' in his memory. In June 1878 he read the lesson at the service in St Peter's Tiverton, and he was Chairman of the Old Boys' Feast. At the relevant point in the proceedings Russell rose to speak, 'which was the signal for long-continued cheering. When this subsided, he told us that Dr Richards, of birchen memory, had taught him very little of anything, and nothing of elocution, he therefore was but a poor speaker. Yet he managed to make us laugh a good deal.' He read the lesson again in 1879. In 1880 the School

Magazine described the gathering on the School Green: 'Once more the kindly face of "owd Passon Jack" beamed on us as hale and fit as ever.' During the after dinner speeches in the School the headmaster, A.L. Francis, said that it was now some years since he had the pleasure of seeing Mr Russell, who was then a good deal older than he is now. His appearance was certainly calculated to prove that the sun could go backwards, or in other words "run to heel". The Rev. John Russell on rising to return thanks was received in a way which cannot be called anything but uproarious. From the youngest boy in the crowded gallery to the most staid looking of the Old Boys all shouted as if they wished to try well the strength of the Armada beams. Mr Russell's speech was in every way characteristic, vigorous, downright and hearty, and his sitting down was the occasion for cheering that would have been as loud as before, had not all been rather exhausted by their efforts.' At a later stage he aptly returned thanks on behalf of the Ladies, looking at them seated to right and left 'How happy could I be with either, Were t'other fair charmer away.' He was present at the Feasts of 1881 and 1882, reading the lesson and making a speech, in one of which he claimed that he had not missed an Old Boys' Day since he had left in 1814.

Russell's friendship with the Luttrells was even more long lived. In December 1876 he had been a guest at the Luttrells and a relation of the Luttrells wrote the following account for Otter Davies, which illustrates Russell's remarkable capacity for friendship. 'On the 28th December 1876 Mr Russell was on a visit to his old college friend, the Rev. A.F. Luttrell of East Quantockshead. On the following day, after going on the Quantock Hills on foot to look for the hounds of Mr Luttrell of Dunster, he went on to St Audries, the seat of Sir Alexander Acland Hood, to dine and to sleep, and to be present at the tenants' ball on the evening of the 29th. During dinner he mentioned as a curious coincidence that, on looking over some old family papers, he found that in the Christmas week of 1776, his father had ridden from Meeth to Dunster to pass a few days at the Castle with his old friend and school fellow Mr Luttrell the then squire of Dunster. Now in the Christmas of 1876, their two sons were passing some days together, both over four score years. At the tenants' ball the same night, Mr Russell was among the most active dancers, joining in quadrilles, lancers and country dances with the prettiest girls in the room, and greeting all his old friends in his hearty manner. He retired to bed at three a.m., regretting the necessity of leaving the scene before the Sir Roger de Coverley began, but he had to start at eight a.m. on a journey of over 40 miles as he had promised Lord Portsmouth to be back soon after twelve to show him his second fox. The previous Monday had been his eighty-first birthday.'

The Luttrells were not the only family where Russell's capacity for friendship can be seen descending the generations. With the Portsmouths, Poltimores, Rolles, and Fortescues he maintained a relationship that started with grandparents and went on to grandchildren. And this was so with the humbler sort too, though it is less easy to document. Before he left Swimbridge he had started the necessary rebuilding of the parish church, using his wide connections to raise the money. In September 1880 he was invited back from Black Torrington for the rededication of the parish church after its restoration at a cost of £2600. The day began with a service in the restored Church, where the congregation was swelled by the attendance of over twenty neighbouring clergy and Bishop Temple of Exeter, who preached. The new incumbent, The Rev. R. Martin 'intoned' the service and Russell read one of the lessons and took the chair in the luncheon that followed. The Bishop had to speak first as he had to leave early for another engagement and in his speech he paid tribute to Russell's work in the parish, 'such unanimity of feeling in the parish...indicates that your late vicar has somehow or other found a way to your hearts in the discharge of his duties. I have always had a very warm regard for him. I have always been ready to recognise in him a very hearty, true, conscientious man, a very warm friend and a very careful doer of all the duties he had undertaken. And now that he has gone away it is a great satisfaction that those who knew him when he was here should be so ready to gather round him on the occasion of the completion of a work which he had taken up with great heartiness, and which he has done so much to bring to its admirable conclusion.' Russell's friend and former neighbour, Mr Smyth, who kept a pack of harriers, proposed the toast of 'The Archdeacon and the Clergy' and included the suggestion that 'Mr Russell was an example to most of those present, and not less to the clergy than to the laity.' Later the Reverend J. Edmonds of Highbray concluded the toast of the 'Chairman' with the words, 'When he should become an old man, which would not be until most of those who were middle-aged had passed away, he would give up hunting, hang his saddle and whip in the church where formerly they placed a gold-laced hat as a prize for wrestling and retire to a hermitage to be built in the hillside at Swimbridge, whence he might emerge now and then to give his benison to the huntsmen as they pursued their quarry. When Mr Russell passes away he will leave behind him one of the sweetest memories ever left by man, and that not for any reason that lay beyond the reach of most of us, for his power to win had been the power simply of the human heart.'

In September 1880 he was certainly not yet an 'old man', except that he was rising eighty-four. In November 1879 he had gone on a tour of the Midland hunts. On November 3rd he was at the opening meet of the Quorn, staying with and mounted by Mr Pennell-Elmhirst. On the 4th he hunted with the Cottesmore and in the evening dined with its master Lord Carington. On the 5th he followed the Belvoir in a carriage. On the 6th he travelled to Bath, on Friday the 7th he saw the Duke of Beaufort's hounds find a fox and left for home hoping to hunt with Lord Portsmouth on the Saturday. In 1881 Anstruther Thompson took Russell and Whyte-Melville, the equally aged father of the author, to all four days of Ascot and reports that the two veterans were the life and soul of the party. In 1881 he also hunted with the stag hounds most vigorously and Nicholas Snow of Oare wrote 'I well remember seeing him as he crossed the moors from Culbone with the leading hounds, and shall never forget his ringing cheer as they broke from the river to Badgery and on to Brendon Common. Several people passed the remark, "Look at Russell, leading across Badgery!"' In September 1881 the *North Devon Journal* reported that Russell had not been wasting his time at Black Torrington. 'When he arrived a hare was no sooner seen in Black Torrington than shot. Mr Russell started a pack of harriers last season; and since that time all landowners for miles around have cheerfully preserved game for his sport. Hounds acknowledge the charm of his manner as readily as men do. Nobody ever showed a similar sympathy with their peculiarities or the same kind of command over them. He carries a horn but seldom needs it; and will not have a whip used. He will let them draw so wide at times that they seem lost to control. His voice, strong and clear as ever, is all that is wanted. Its stentorian tones may be heard a good mile off, and to it every one of his pack will fly in an instant. To spend a day with the great hunting parson and his harriers is a pleasure for which any true sportsman would cheerfully give up the most brilliant run with other hounds. At dinner afterwards he will be found as genial and entertaining a companion as one need desire; brimful of good Devonshire stories, which he tells with a mastery of the dialect that is inimitable.'

However when he attended the stag hounds in the autumn of 1882 all was obviously far from well. He was due to go up to London to officiate at a wedding, but was too ill to attempt the journey. Short stays at East Anstey and Bude in search of recovery availed nothing. The Prince of Wales desired to be kept informed of this progress and sent gifts of game and mutton. On April 28th, 1883, very peacefully he died. His body was taken by funeral train to Swimbridge for burial. The Prince of Wales sent a wreath and a letter to the family, mourning Russell 'as a friend'. Apart from family and local gentry, the press named 24 clergy as attending, as well as the Mayors of South Molton and Barnstaple. The church was packed and it was estimated that over a thousand thronged the churchyard. The Archdeacon of Exeter later quoted the following: 'At his funeral the entire neighbourhood was gathered, clergy, squires, farmers, young and old, all sorts and conditions of men; and amongst them, not a few of the gypsy tribe whom he often met when riding to the meet. They used to bring their children to him to be baptised, and regarded him as a kind of patron of their class. As the great concourse moved away from the graveside, a farmer was asked what he thought was the secret of this widespread appeal. "Oh, sir," he said, "he wasn't very much of a parson, you know, in the way of visiting and such like; but he was such a man to make peace in a parish." And then he told the tale of a chance meeting with Mr Russell on the roadside, of the turning of the horse's head in consequence of a conversation which then took place, of a visit paid to a sick man's bed, and a reconciliation brought about between a nephew and a dying uncle by a few plain words of homely kindness and common-sense.'

These are the grounds for regarding 'Passon' Jack as one of the great parish clergy of the nineteenth century.

APPENDIX I
Letters from the Heart

As readers of the preface know I have been researching Jack Russell off and on for many years, starting with the unfavourable, almost churlish, opinion of him that I had learnt from Hoskins, that his career was 'futile'. By the time I was ready to write the last two chapters my views on Russell had changed, so that I was prepared to suggest that he was one of the great parish priests of the nineteenth century in his own right, and that, pace Phillpotts, his fame as a sportsman probably assisted his effectiveness as a parson. While seeking illustrations for this book I met Sir Rivers Carew, the inheritor of Sir Walter Palk's baronetcy, who very kindly showed me a bundle of letters from Russell to his great-grandmother, Mrs Lock Roe, who had lived at The Manor House, Lynmouth, a few hours ride across Exmoor from the Russells at Swimbridge. Mrs Lock Roe was born in St Austell, Cornwall in 1838 and her first names were Mary Theresa and her husband, Robert Roe, was one of three sons of the Reverend Thomas Roe of Brendon on Exmoor, who had married a Mary Lock in 1804. The eldest son of the Reverend Thomas was called John Colwell Roe, mentioned by Russell in his diary in 1824, who died without issue in the late 1850s as Lord of the Manors of Lyn and Countisbury. Robert was the third son and in the 1851 census described himself as a Master Mariner, which probably explains the fact that the birth of his eldest daughter Ada occurred on a ship in New Zealand waters. In 1863 and 1864 two further daughters were born, Theresa and Frances. So when the first letter was written Russell was seventy-six and Mary Lock Roe, or Mie, as he called her, was thirty-three and her husband Robert about sixty years old. Looking up 'mie' in a French dictionary may give the equivalent of 2+2 = 22, as it means 'my dearest', 'darling' or 'honey'. Yet I have not the slightest doubt that the relationship, though strongly emotional, was entirely proper. Too many of us have lost the knack of emotional, loving, but sexually chaste relationships with the opposite sex.

With Sir Rivers' permission I am presenting a selection of the letters because they glow with the old man's humanity. Russell did not always date his letters, so sometimes I have had to rely on the postmark, not always a reliable guide as all the envelopes are the same size and it is clear that, over the years, letters may have been replaced in the 'wrong' envelopes. When transcribing these letters I have done my best to be faithful to Russell's punctuation.

The first letter seems to be Christmas 1871, written while he was a guest of the Earl of Portsmouth at Eggesford. Mrs Lock Roe's husband, Robert, is obviously ill.

'My dear Mie,

I have been, as usual, spending my birthday [Dec 21st] at Eggesford, which will, I hope, plead my excuse for having so long neglected to thank you for your last letter, for tho' it contained anything but good news of the health of my dear old friend Robert, still I hope that the change from Devon to London will make it all right with him. We have, all of us, some bother to contend with, but I have little fear about your husband's future,– he has brooded too much over, what some other men would not have considered, troubles, annoying as they must have been, and this circumstance has made him all wrong - give my love to him and tell him that he shall have a long letter from me, full of news, in a few days – now I am up to my hocks, for I had 43 letters out of 45 received within a few days, to answer yesterday morning! My birthday. The clock has just struck twelve- Xmas Day, or rather Christmas night, – so I must be off to my 'feathers', or the old woman will be singing out for 'John Russell'. With best love to you both, and hearty good wishes that, if your Xmas be not a merry one, the New Year may be a happier one than the last.

I am, my dear, yours very affectionately, J. Russell.'

The second letter he dated from Dennington on December 10th, 1873.

'My dear Mie,

I am returned from Norfolk and none the worse for my introduction to His Royal Highness!!!, for he invited me to his Ball,– to which I went, and came straight,– or rather without stopping,– to this house from Sandringham after it was over! The Princess is a lovely little creature, and told me she loved hunting as much as I did- Query! I go there again on the 31st of this month and remain 'till the following Monday, taking the Church duty on the Sunday – People say I shall soon be the Arch-Bishop of Canterbury!! Tell Mrs Whitehead of my prospective good fortune with my kindest regards! I shall ride down and see you both, I hope, before I go, – but the Missus will keep me to her side day and night. Mary Taylor is to be married – by me – in St James' Chapel on the 6th of next month – the day after I leave Sandringham – I hope they will be very happy, but they can't know much of each other yet. The Duke of Hamilton and Lady Mary Montague – who are to be married to-day – were at the Ball with the Duke and Duchess of Manchester, her father and mother. She looked larky, and her daughter plain– No more hunting for some time, I fear, for 'tis very cold and frosty. Kind love from us both to yourself and the dear little young ones – Ever yours, dear, very affectionately J. Russell.'

It must be remembered that the next letter is from a man of seventy-nine years, of blameless reputation. What it shows is his extraordinary vigour, the sensitivity of his heart and the grace of his turn of phrase. It was probably written from a friend's house in Ivybridge, or from Marley, the Carew house on the southern fringes of Dartmoor. Its humanity annihilates time, a lonely old man, whose wife was very ill, writing to a lonely mother, anxious about the health and soundness of mind of her husband.

'March 25th, 1874.

In my bed room – all alone, alone, alas! 12 o'clock at night – before a good fire – very lonely!

My dear Mie,

I got your letter this morning – but I am here for the week, I cannot go to you. We are hunting every day with Mr Rolle's and Mr Trelawny's Hounds – on Monday and Tuesday we had two good days with Mr Rolle, killing on the open moor on Monday, and earthling in view yesterday. Today Trelawney has done nothing except earthing two heavy vixens. So next, – we have a houseful here – Lord Morley and his sister Lady Catherine Parker, Mr Rolle and Lady Gertrude, two Mr Corytons, Mr Michell, whom you don't know, and myself. Dinner parties everyday. Miss Glanville has dined here today and we sat next each other at dinner, and talk'd of you "long and anxiously as lovers write to one another". Did your face burn, – dear– about 8 o' clock? I can't hunt next week, the following is Easter week. I shall be very glad to be your chaperon anywhere – with the "Stars" or "Garters". The Missus was getting better when I left her, but she is still a cripple, and suffers much from rheumatism. Fanny Riccard [a niece] is with her now. Good night, my dear Mie, soft and sweet slumbers to you is the wish of yours very affectionately,

J. Russell.

Kiss the babes for me, and I will repay you at sight.'

In the summer of 1874 Robert Lock Roe died. The news of his death brought an instant response

'Monday morning.

Your sad, sad news, my very dear Friend, has quite overpower'd me! I said many times to Mrs Russell yesterday – "No news today will be heartrending news tomorrow, I fear", and so it has turn'd out.

May God have mercy on your poor dear, – and he was indeed dear to us, and to many, many more of his friends' husband's widow and three

fatherless children. All I can say further now is that I will ride over tomorrow or Wednesday. God help you all, – always and for ever.
Your most affectionate
J. Russell.'

And also a letter from Penelope Russell, whose handwriting is identical with that of her father, the Admiral, and who, like her husband, at seventy-five years has all her wits about her and has a sharp turn of phrase, especially about husbands, dead or alive. That she also calls Mary Roe 'Mie' is significant, probably everyone did.
'Dennington, June 11th 1874,
My dear Mie,
I did not deserve your kind letter this morning and think it so good of you to make any thing like an excuse for [my] not writing to you as I ought to have done!
I am sure you will believe me when I say no-one can have felt the loss of a valued friend more than I have done for your dear husband; he was always, as you know, an especial favourite of mine from my long knowledge of his upright conduct, gentlemanly feeling and right judgement in most things! Lynmouth will never be the same place without his honest face, which I should miss more than I can express! Though a little warm weather may set me up, and enable me to mingle our grief at the irreparable loss you have sustained.
My old man did not go to Bodmin, as he proposed, this morning. I was so wretchedly ill the whole night, he did not like to leave me, added to which the weather was not tempting for a ride, on an old screw, of nearly 70 miles! He now means to start by 3 o'clock to-morrow morning......
With love to yourself and kisses to the dear children,
believe me yours
very affectionately
P.Russell.'

The next two letters are both from 1875, in spite of the fact that Russell, in his agitation, misdated the first, as we are all inclined to do in early January.
'Dennington, Jan 2nd 1874.
My dear Mie,
Would that I could be,– or rather that my letter were – the bearer of good, instead of bad, news to you – but it has pleased the Almighty to take – as I hope and believe – to his own holy keeping my dear Wife and faithful and loving friend thro' a period of nearly 49 years. She breathed her last yesterday afternoon about 2 o'clock peacefully, and, I believe, painlessly, for which I humbly thank my God. I

cannot write more to you now – but I shall have much to say when we meet. With best love and every good wish to yourself and children for the New Year, ever

My dear Friend

Yrs most affectionately

J. Russell.'

And the other is probably from the summer of 1875

'Monday morning,

My dear Mie,

I confess that I have been negligent, but not forgetful of even one of the damsels, – I suppose your sex is not changed tho' you are a widow – now located in the Manor House of Lynmouth, and therefore you must forgive my negligence. We shall meet I hope on Wednesday in the Show Field – and then we'll settle something about my looking you up under your own roof tree. I am very seedy, very lonely and any thing but very happy!

Ever, dear, yours

affectionately

J. Russell.'

By 1876 Russell was taking more interest in life as he prepared to move out of Dennington in favour of his son, Bury, and move himself to Tordown. Lionel Bencraft was his nephew.

'Dennington, March 2nd, 1876.

My dear Mie,

I am here all alone, for Mary [his housekeeper] is gone to Tordown with a lot of glass etc etc, and weak as water with an attack of d........a! I have been seedy all the week, and for many days before it commenced, but hope to be well enough to ride down to Ivybridge on Monday and see all the sport the two packs – Coryton's and the Dartmoor – can shew me. My billet will be Delamere – Admiral Parker's – where I shall meet Lady Katherine Parker – you will remember riding by her side from Cloutsham to Watersmeet, where the hounds killed their stag – some few – how many I forget – years ago. I don't think I shall return for a fortnight, but go on to Scorrier and see a meet with the Four Barrow Hounds near to the Land's End, a spot I never yet beheld. I must ride all the way, for I cannot stand training Horses! Mary will transport all the furniture, or nearly all, while I am away, and Bury and his people will take possession of this house before Ladyday. I shall not be sorry to go, for the loneliness of the long evenings makes me, at times, very sad, and, unless people are staying in the House, my visitors, morning or evening, can be easily counted. I am glad you like the 'fresh importation' [a governess?] – if the children – I beg Ada's pardon!

– 135 –

are also fond of her, they will be sure to 'get forward' under her tuition. When I return from Cornwall you will soon have to give me one of your old 'Highland Welcomes'. Lionel and his wife dined here yesterday – she is helping Mary most kindly about the furniture etc etc – arranging what shall be taken to Tordown and what left here, and as I have not, and do not intend to interfere with any arrangements they may make, no ill feeling can arise in the minds of either Father or Son on the subject relating thereto! Well now, my dear Mie, I must toddle upstairs and begin packing my Sermons, Books etc etc – for the masons and carpenters want to come into my dressing rooms. So fare thee well – dear – and best love to you all – all whom I know of your household!. Believe me yours very affectionately

J. Russell.'

The next letter reflects Russell's remarkable appetite for life and dates from only a few days before his eighty-fifth birthday.
'Tordown, 10th November, 1879

Mrs Pyke Nott came downstairs for the first time for many months past. Have just left her, they all go to Bath next week. Only a hasty line, my dear Mie, to thank you for your very kind invitation for this week, but I cannot leave home again, for I only returned from Leicestershire and Bath last Friday night, after having hunted with five packs of Foxhounds during the week – the Quorn, the Cottesmore, the Duke of Rutland's, the Duke of Beaufort's and on Saturday with Lord Portsmouth's. I'm now just returned from the Traveller's Rest School, whither I went this morning to meet the Inspector!! Bah!

I hope to meet Nicholas at Parracombe tomorrow, and heartily wish you could do the same. [Perhaps Nicholas Snow of Oare and a hunting engagement.] With best and kindest love to you all. Believe me
Yours very affectionately,
J. Russell.
The Browns and Baileys are walking upwards and I have 40 letters to answer!'

This is a letter from Christmas a month later and shows his sadness upon leaving his beloved Swimbridge.
'Tordown, 29th December, 1879.
My dear Mie,
Many, very many thanks for all your kind and good wishes. I shall ride over and spend the day with you the first moment that I can, but my time is occupied with answering letters – I have had almost 50 since the 20th, my birthday is the 21st, as you know – and riding and driving to Black Torrington and back. Bah! how I hate the word, for I cannot bear to leave this my little happy home.

Poor dear Mrs Riddle! What a good, dear kind soul she was – and how warmly she always welcom'd me whenever and wherever we met. I deeply lament her loss – but it is 'appointed' to us all to die! I have no time to write more than to offer you all my best and warmest wishes for the New Year, and to assure you, my dear Mie, that I am and ever shall be,

    Yours very affectionately,
    J. Russell.'

And the last is the surviving fragment of probably his final letter to Mie and dates from 1882. The 'troubles' refer to the collapse of Bury's Bank and the breakdown of Bury's health.

'… My visit to Sandringham was a very pleasant one, all my visits there have been so from the first, every one gives them the same character, and every one is happy, as happy as I was there. The Prince and Princess – conjointly – gave me a Diamond Scarf Pin, and he placed it in my scarf himself, and, on leaving, they each held me by my hands and said "you will take care of it, won't you?". I need not recapitulate my reply. Nor need I tell you of all the troubles that have befallen the House of Russell since we last met, for you must know most of them – but I hope, as Bury's mind must be now somewhat at rest, his bodily pains will be lessen'd. He has gone through a roughish ordeal, poor fellow and I hope I shall pull through mine. With my best love to yourself and all the Bairns, believe me,

    My dear Mie
    Yours very affectionately, J. Russell.'

And so, a few months later, both father and son slipped into the darkness.

APPENDIX II
Poems

In his life Russell was the subject of a considerable body of verse and the following are three specimens. The first is by his mentor George Templer and is extracted from a much longer poem called 'A Party at Stover', dating from 1823. The first verse and the verse referring to Russell were:

> Ye gentlemen sportsmen, whosoever ye be,
> That delight in hexameters, listen to me: –
> I sing of a party assembled at Stover,
> To hunt in the morning, and feast when 'twas over;
> All spirits determined as e'er followed a fox,
> On Dartmoor's wild mountains through morasses and rocks.

> …Another prime minister rode from the North,
> Of his talents Southmolton can best tell the worth,
> So prone to the chase that he followed each scent,
> From the stag in the forest to' bubble a vent';
> More attached to his bed than a lover of wine,
> He was sure to be sound on his pillow by nine.

The second poem is a tribute to the Earl of Portsmouth's Eggesford Hunt and was written in 1860 and is 32 verses long. After a description of the pack and praise of the family there are verses in extolling the virtues of members of the hunt, no less than 11 of whom are clergymen. But only Russell gets more than one verse, which, in the light of the letters in Appendix 1, interestingly refers to his gallantry towards the ladies.

> Whoever you are you must ride in a bustle
> If you e'er shew your stern to famous Jack Russell,
> For in preaching and hunting his peer I don't know.
> And the text he loves best is a sweet 'Tally-Ho'.

> But strong as the voice in the rostrum may be,
> Or shrill as a curlew when streaming o'er lea,

It can mellow in sooth that most prepotent cheer,
And soften its accents to, 'Not so, my dear.'

To Prince and to Commoner, one and the same,
Gives due praise to merit, as ready to blame;
If his eye is too keen to be ever caught dozing,
So free is his tongue from the business of glozing.

In forest or palace, in cot as in boudoir,
With the fox in the gorse, or with 'grande Dame au parloir'
'Tis well to be hero, top sawyer, or what not,
Ever cock of the walk, and, o'er all, fly your top-knot.

No critic can pretend these are great poetry, but the third is a touching
tribute from a native of Swimbridge to commemorate the centenary of
Russell's death. No-one can travel in North Devon today without real-
ising that, among the 'natives' the name of Russell is green and sweet.
This poetic tribute by Marvyn Dalling, Swimbridge's chronicler, is
useful in that it reminds the reader of the two chapels of ease that were
built to serve the more far flung parts of the parish in Russell's ministry.
Schools were also built and overseen by the parson as one of the letters
in Appendix 1 records. It is from the heart and speaks for itself and is
designed to be sung to 'Clementine':

PARSON JACK

Once there was a country parson,
Who in Swymbridge did reside;
And his work within that parish
Is remembered still with pride.
  And his name? It was John Russell;
  Better known as 'Parson Jack',
  Spent his leisure hours out hunting,
  With his very famous pack.

Faithfully he worked his parish;
Built a Church at Traveller's Rest;
He performed his many duties
With great energy and zest.
  And his name? It was Jack Russell, etc

His concern for all the needy;
Some were sick, and some were poor,
Made him plead from many pulpits

For the rich to help them more.
    And his name? It was Jack Russell, etc

He had friends in highest places,
Even Edward, Prince of Wales;
And was loved by humble gypsies
Camping in the local vales.
    And his name? It was Jack Russell, etc

He another Church erected,
'Twas 'The Holy Name' at Gunn;
So we know this famous Parson
Worked as well as had his fun.
    And his name? It was Jack Russell, etc

Forty-eight years spent at Swymbridge,
Then Black Torrington for three;
He was called to highest heaven,
With his Maker, there to be.
    And his name? It was Jack Russell, etc

He's remembered for his hunting
And the dogs that bear his name;
He enjoyed his work and leisure, –
  We must try to do the same.
    And his name? It was Jack Russell, etc.

BIBLIOGRAPHY

Memoir of the Rev. John Russell and his Out-of-Door Life by E.W.L. Davies, M.A. 1878, updated 1883 and reprinted 1902.
In his preface Davies stated that 'the proof sheets of every chapter were submitted to Mr Russell himself that any statement might be corrected by his own hand'. It is an invaluable record of what Russell wanted remembered about himself, but his memory was that of an eighty-three-year-old and not always correct.

Eighty Years' Reminiscences by Colonel Anstruther Thomson, 1904.
'Jack' Anstruther Thomson was a wealthy Lowland laird who was a famous horseman and Meltonian. He devoted a chapter to Russell and produced a useful clutch of letters from Russell to himself. Like Davies, Thomson produces a rather bland image of Russell

Hunting Parson by Lady Eleanor Kerr, 1963.
Very useful on the terriers. She quotes from poems that I have therefore omitted.

Letters on the Past and Present Foxhounds of Devonshire by C.A.H., 1861.
The C.A.H stands for Charles Arthur Mohun Harris of Hayne House, Stowford, Russell's friend of the Iddesleigh years and the creator of St Hubert's Hall. Harris gives a useful record of the Stover years of George Templer and records the importance of the young Russell in the annals of Devonshire fox hunting. Rather hagiographical.

Combat and Carnival by Peter Carew, 1962.
A fund of stories about Russell and his relationship with Sir Walter Palk Carew of Haccombe. The portrait of Sir Walter is richly comic, but is based on the diaries of the women in his family. Which paterfamilias would like posterity to learn about himself solely from such sources? Sir Walter and a Fortescue married sisters whose beauty was legendary. I suspect Sir Walter was more peripheral to Russell's life, who may have preferred the company of Lady Carew and her sister.

Nineteenth Century Magazines.
Bailey's Magazine, the *Sporting Magazine*, the *Gentleman's Magazine* and others have been perused. They give details of the major sporting

events and are a guide to Russell's fame and major hunting activities. It is clear that at the latest from the 1840s their readers knew who Russell was in the same way that modern readers of the sports pages would know who Botham was.

Devon Newspapers.
Barnstaple and North Devon were blessed by two newspapers the *North Devon Journal*, which reported things in a fiercely Liberal way and the *Advertiser* which was truly Tory. Invaluable for details of Russell's parochial life and non-hunting activities.

Russell's Diaries.
These are basically a record of his hunting activities although the diaries for 1824-6 have helped to unravel his wooing and winning of Penelope Incledon Bury. He had a beautiful hand, but only rarely bared his soul. Russell's private papers have been scattered, perhaps because of his death and that of his son, Bury, coming together in 1883. I suspect that there was once a complete sequence of 'hunting diaries' from the early 1830s to the late 1850s. More may turn up.

Other Documents.
Parochial Records of the parishes he served attest to the dutifulness with which he approached his calling. Scraps of Bishop Phillpotts' diary tell that, initially, Phillpotts had a warm regard for Russell. Sale particulars of the 'big houses' he visited were useful as were the Land Tax records of the early nineteenth century in showing who owned what and how much.

MAP OF DEVON

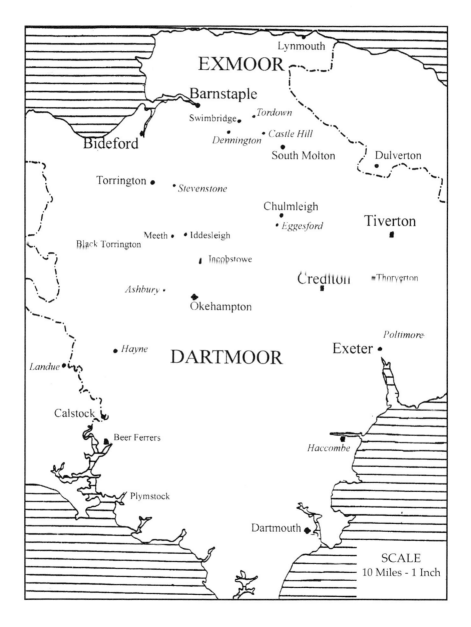

Lynmouth

EXMOOR

Barnstaple

Swimbridge • •Tordown

Dennington • • Castle Hill

South Molton

Bideford

Dulverton

Torrington •

•Stevenstone

Chulmleigh

Tiverton

•Eggesford

Meeth • •Iddesleigh

Black Torrington

•Inpobstowe

Crediton •Thorverton

Ashbury •

Okehampton

•Hayne

DARTMOOR

Poltimore

Exeter •

Landue •

Calstock

Beer Ferrers

Haccombe

Plymstock

Dartmouth •

SCALE
10 Miles - 1 Inch

INDEX